PROHIBITED
PROFITS

PROHIBITED PROFITS

BY
SETH MANISCALCO

FOREWORD BY
DAVID MELTZER

The first step to changing your financial future and guaranteeing your families future is to make a decision. Are you committed to securing your piece of the Prohibited Profits opportunity?

Over the years I've met thousands of people that understand how to make money. Today, there is no shortage of business gurus and financial experts. Very few understand wealth creation and living a life of abundance like Seth Maniscalco.

It took me years to realize that life was about more than money. Life is about living in pursuit of our potential through serving others, starting with our family. I grew up with limiting beliefs about money.

Since I was a little kid, it was ingrained in me that money and happiness were linked. Growing up with a single mother, who raised six kids with very minimal support from my father, the only times that I ever saw my beloved mom unhappy were when she was having financial issues.

When the car would break down or the dishwasher needed to be replaced, I saw the strain that it would put on my mother, and I resolved myself to be "rich" in the future. I wanted to be rich enough to buy my mom a house and a car, so that she wouldn't have to worry about those aspects of her life anymore.

As I progressed through my career, something rather unfortunate happened…. I became successful. Things like becoming a millionaire just nine months out of law school, running Samsung's first smartphone division, and serving as CEO of the renowned Leigh Steinberg Sports & Entertainment agency helped to reinforce my belief that money brought happiness.

The more success I saw, the further away I got from the values which had brought me success in the first place (gratitude, empathy, accountability, and effective communication). I did end up meeting my goal of buying my mom a house and car but failed to realize that I had lost touch with myself along the way.

I became convinced that money could buy happiness and that mindset nearly ended up costing me everything, but one event changed everything. Having become entitled and lost touch with my values, I had decided to lie to my wife one night about having to work and instead I went to an Emmys Party with the rapper Lil Jon.

When I came home drunk, she told me that she was unhappy with me and who I had become. Blinded by my success, I resolved to leave her and take all of her happiness away. When I awoke in the morning, I was angry and prepared to follow through with my resolution. In that moment I looked in the closet and spotted a jacket that my father had given me.

You see, despite leaving my mom, my father had been my hero growing up, until he forgot my 10th birthday and decided to lie. He told me he hadn't forgotten my birthday; he simply didn't celebrate them. It was a devastating blow to our relationship and something that I didn't get over until decades later.

The next gift I got from my father was on my 30th birthday, when he sent me a custom jacket. I was elated to finally get a gift and hoped that this would be the first step in mending our relationship, then I looked closer at the jacket. The pockets had all been ripped out, so I called my father to ask why he was torturing me with this damaged jacket.

His message was clear: he told me the jacket was not for me to wear, it was a reminder. The jacket with no pockets was meant to remind me that you can't take anything with you when you die. It had taken my father twenty years to learn that lesson, and he wanted to pass it along to me.

I kept that jacket in my closet and didn't pay it much attention, until the morning after the Emmy Awards fiasco. When I woke up that next morning, I was still angry at my wife for calling me out the evening before. It wasn't until I set eyes upon that jacket hanging in my closet that I realized just how lost I was.

I had been living in a world of scarcity, chasing profits rather than living in abundance, as I consistently and persistently enjoy my pursuit of my potential. This experience helped me to shift my perspective in a massive way.

The lessons that Seth shares in this book will help you to shed that scarce mindset holding you back, as well as to take concrete actions towards your wealth goals. Don't just dream about manifesting your goals, you need to put into practice what my friend John Assaraf calls the Law of GOYA (Get Off Your Ass!).

Prohibited Profits lays out strategies to help you be happier where you are financially, as well as helping you angle towards where you want to be in terms of building your wealth.

Prohibited Profits is not just a message about creating wealth. It is a path to help you leverage your time, so that you can continue down the path of pursuing your highest potential. For people like myself and Seth, that means leveraging wealth to create freedom to show up as a better father, husband and leader.

This book will help you learn from history and unlock the secrets of wealth hidden from the masses. Prohibited Profits will teach you how to locate opportunities and how to take massive action immediately. Remember, our intentions don't work unless we work. They law of GOYA is the only way to create the life of your dreams. When you take the right actions with your money and can combine that with the currency of faith, you are certain to end up somewhere better, brighter, and richer.

CONTENTS

CHAPTER 1

PROHIBITED SYSTEMS

They say that every man has two lives, and the second starts when he realizes he has just one. I remember that phrase because my first life doesn't seem that long ago.

I will never forget the pain I felt, working 100-hour weeks on the road 40+ weeks per year working for Siemens Medical. Even to this day, I cringe thinking about calling my kids late at night just so I could say goodnight. All I ever wanted to be was an amazing father. The best way I knew how to be an amazing father was to provide for them financially.

Growing up, that was how I was told the world worked. I was sold the American dream. I knew if I could climb the corporate ladder long enough, eventually I would reach financial freedom. The American dream felt more like an impossible myth.

The myth of the American dream was firmly planted in my militant mind. If I just worked hard enough and long enough, I could retire with enough money in the bank. If I was lucky, I might have enough left to enjoy the latter years of my life. I had a 401K, stock options and retirement accounts. By all accounts, I was living the American dream. Only it was purgatory for me. I was trapped and it was costing me my freedom.

Sure, I was making a 6-figure salary which I didn't take for-granted. But I certainly didn't feel free and there was no extra time to enjoy the fruits of my labor. I kept telling myself this was the only way and I had to keep going.

But where did I learn those myths? Why was I following the same American dream that failed my parents a generation earlier?

These were conditioned beliefs I learned growing up in a working-class family. I remember when I was 6 years old, my parents moved us out of their apartment and into our first home. It was a $50,000 house and it was everything they could afford after years of chasing their own American dream.

The house was old, and to put it nicely, it was a trainwreck. But it was home and they spent their lives working to afford it.

Me? I was a latchkey kid growing up. My mom was a secretary, and my dad was working 60-hour weeks. I never saw my parents until late at night and it got me into trouble, trying to manage life for myself at a young age.

It also taught me a lot about life, and I stumbled into business lessons that still serve me today. I found myself starting my first business when I was 16 years old. It wasn't business that 16-year-old me should have been building, but I was a young entrepreneur in training.

I remember taking a job at McDonalds working for $5.25/hour. I put everything I had into that job. After 90 days, my boss sat me down and shared some encouraging feedback...

"Seth, we are so excited about you! You were our best employee for the first couple months, and we would like to give you a raise."

Already planning what I would do with my newly found wealth, I said, "thank you, how much?"

"7 cents Seth, that's above standard for a first raise"

"WHAT THE #$^*" I thought to myself. I had just put everything I had into this job and what did I have to show for it? A 7-cent raise. I quit almost immediately. I didn't know what the alternative plan would be at the time, but it wasn't going to be 7-cent raises. I knew that much.

It was a difficult, but important lesson because it made me angry. It forced me to find alternative solutions.

At the time, that solution was marijuana. Today, marijuana is everywhere, decriminalized and studies have shown its medical benefits. However, this was during the Ronald Reagan days. Weed was very illegal and stigmatized. Videos spread across televisions depicting brains frying like egg yolks.

Marijuana… was… bad!

But everyone I knew seemed to like it and I was sick of 7 cent raises. It became my first business. Although I may not have been proud of being a law breaker at the time, it was the first time I understood the concept of Prohibited Profits.

It didn't seem so bad to me. I was making money hand over fist. My customers were happy, and I learned the important concept of supply and demand. I was on fire, unstoppable and on track.

Only the law didn't like my business, I ended up in trouble and eventually, I found my way into the U.S Marines. A place that molded me into the man I am today. It was the Marines that helped me find confidence and discipline that has fueled my success.

The Marines gave me a different perspective and identity than the one I had at home. At home I was a troublemaker and weed dealer. The world convinced me that something was wrong with me. In the Marines, I was a leader and my leadership qualities were valued. I realized that my self-worth wasn't based on what someone at home thought of me.

I look back on those days and still struggle, feeling like I wasn't actually doing anything wrong. Jay Z and Mark Wahlberg got their start the same way, so why did I feel guilty? Why did I feel like I was doing something wrong?

Later in life, I realized the patterns. A pattern of regulations created by our government to control society. They wanted to make the rules. If you follow the money today, it's easy to understand why.

If something doesn't fit into their box, it becomes illegal. No deaths were ever recorded from overdosing on marijuana. Yet, 29 states outlawed marijuana between 1916-1931. Conveniently, that was right around the time the U.S. government put a nationwide constitutional ban on the production, importation, transportation and sale of alcoholic beverages.

Better referred to as alcohol prohibition. If you are recognizing the patterns, you are already seeing with one eye open.

During hearings on marijuana law in the 1930's, claims were made about marijuana. They said that it had the ability to cause men of color to become violent and solicit sex from white women. This imagery became the backdrop for the Marijuana Tax Act of 1937. That Act effectively banned its use and sales.

By the 1970's, Cannabis was placed in the most restrictive category, a schedule 1 substance. President Nixon did nothing to change that law or advance research.

The short history lesson isn't meant to convince you to start or invest in marijuana, alcohol or anything else the government deems bad. The lesson is meant to flip the script on our perception of right. I want you to understand the rules that were created to keep us stuck on the U.S. government hamster wheel.

It is also an opportunity for you to recognize the patterns of history. If you understand history, you can take advantage of current opportunities in the marketplace. Alcohol was bad, until the government figured out how to get their cut. Marijuana was bad, until 1996 when California approved it. Then it became a powerful revenue generator for the state's growth.

Since then, other states have followed. But no other state has taken advantage of the opportunity quite like California and Colorado.

I call it first movers' advantage. If you can recognize what is being currently denied by society, you can take advantage of these opportunities for yourself. Especially if you can spot trends that will eventually become mainstream.

Whether you are an accredited investor new to investment or have just wanted to find a way to capitalize on modern shifts in wealth during these difficult times.

You already know how difficult, yet important it is to stay notified and up to date on relevant data, make decisions without emotions and be able to practically predict the future.

Most people already know that 1% of the population holds 98% of the wealth. There are only a few opportunities in each lifetime, to join those ranks.

This book, Prohibited Profits shares how you can learn from history and gives you proven modern day strategies to capture wealth and secure a fortune that will outlive you and your ancestors.

These patterns are not just limited to alcohol and cannabis. Prohibition and government control has been happening since the beginning of governments.

In fact, these patterns have shaped our economy forever.

In 1913, Woodrow Wilson passed the Federal Reserve Act. This gave the government more control over the nation's banking infrastructure.

The Glass-Steagall Act of 1933 created the Federal Deposit Insurance Corporation (FDIC). This implemented regulation of deposit interest rates and separated commercial from investment banking.

The Banking Act of 1935 served to strengthen and give the Federal Reserve more centralized power.

Even modern-day investing was limited and controlled by the government and the 1% wealthy. Until recently, angel investing was only open to accredited investors. Meaning if you didn't have a liquid net worth of $1 million, excluding your primary residence, you couldn't invest in startups.

That meant the average person couldn't invest in Facebook, Uber, Tesla during the dot.com boom.

These regulations were put in place for one reason.

The government wants control.

Regulations were set up so the government and the 1% have control every step of the way. They want to depict the idea of the American dream. They know that if we, the people, believe we have real opportunity, we will stay on the hamster wheel of success forever.

That is hamster wheel I had found myself on for years. All while I watched my oldest two children grow into adults. I missed most of their childhood because I had fallen for the American trap, disguised as the American dream.

My lens on life changed when my company was sold, and I was promoted to management. I was forced to look at life from that same lens, upside down.

A promotion to management! The American dream was alive and well!

Only the vision for the company had changed. It was no longer about the medical products that were saving people's lives, it was about the money.

I had justified spending all of those hours away from my family because I knew the products were saving lives. I also knew the paycheck was paying the bills back home.

I knew there had to be a better way and I wasn't going to spend my entire life, sacrificing my life for a paycheck. That's when I started to realize these patterns of history. I spent the next 10 years learning commodities and trading markets.

fter discovering those patterns, I noticed a new emerging trend. There was, and still is, a huge problem happening with our governments federal reserve. Our cash reserves were dwindling. On top of that, the federal reserve was diving deeper and deeper into debt. The government was literally printing money out of thin air with nothing to back it.

That has created a huge problem and it's becoming more significant. In 2020 and 2021, we saw trillions of dollars emerge from thin air by way of emergency stimulus packages. While I believe that we should help the American people, money isn't supposed to appear from thin air.

Somebody has to pay for that money, and that somebody may eventually be US, the people.

Imagine waking up one day and having 1/10th of your money evaporate because the government needs your help now. Unfair? Yes. Unconstitutional? Maybe. Impossible? No. Just ask the people of Cyprus who saw this happen in 2013 during the European financial crisis.

We have all become familiar with the phrase "bail out," but there is a real future possibility of a potential "bail in." The fed is printing money with no backing. Eventually, somebody will have to pay the debt.

Enter cryptocurrency, an ally I found while trading the commodities markets. At the time, cryptocurrency and Bitcoin were far from mainstream. Bitcoin was mocked by almost everyone besides the serious early adopters. While I wasn't one of the first movers in 2009, I did start to recognize the patterns early enough.

Bitcoin was a finite currency, meaning there was only so many Bitcoin. You can't print more Bitcoin. Sure, it was a digital currency and mainstream media dismissed its application at the time.

However, as an investor, Bitcoin made perfect sense to me. The opportunity had less to do with the currency itself. It was a solution to the problem patterns that have repeated themselves for the last 150 years.

The U.S. government has a lot to lose by Bitcoin succeeding. The same scenario happened with banking, alcohol, cannabis and investing prohibition eras. Only this time I was in position to take advantage of the opportunity.

I cashed out every dollar from my retirement accounts. I did something bold. If I didn't believe in my retirement accounts, I wasn't going to play it safe. I put my entire 401K l into Bitcoin while it was trading under $250 per share. Depending on when you are reading this, Bitcoin has climbed tremendously, and I see no end in sight.

However, this book isn't a book about Bitcoin, cryptocurrency or any one thing in particular. It's about spotting opportunities before the masses so you can capitalize on first movers' advantage.

We are currently living through the most significant economic shift in U.S. history. Those who spot the opportunities, can build a multi-generational dynasty for themselves. Most importantly, you can set up future generations and create financial freedom for your family.

This book is about locating those opportunities and taking advantage of them. Ultimately, it's also about keeping more of your money in your pocket. You can accomplish all of this by understanding the rules of the game. A game that the establishment doesn't want you to know.

So why a book and why now? Originally, I was going to title this book the 500 Year Plan. For me, financial freedom is about creating a dynasty of sovereignty for my family. A foundational legacy that will live on beyond my children and their children.

A legacy I take so seriously because of the years I lost chasing the myth of the American dream. The years I would have loved to have spent with my parents growing up and the years I wish I had with my now grown children.

Today, I have four kids, two of them young and it feels like a rebirth as a father and a husband. I spend my days trading the markets because that's what I love to do. Most of my trades are systemized because of the processes I have set up in my life. They allow me to spend time doing what I love doing most which is being a dad.

That is true freedom and the real American dream that you won't find in your 401K retirement plan. 10-12% returns are just enough to keep you trapped on the hamster wheel. They want you to keep running until you are 65, or 67 or whatever age the U.S. government decides next.

This book isn't about buying flashy Lamborghinis. If you're looking for stock picks, this is the wrong book for you. This is a book about foundational principles that have allowed me to spot opportunities in any industry.

My portfolio includes everything from cryptocurrency, tree farms and a pistachio farm in Colorado. Prohibited Profits is a timeless message that will allow you to understand and capitalize on opportunities when you recognize them.

Prohibited Profits is about locating those 1000%+ upside opportunities now, so that you're able to enjoy life. I want you to enjoy life, while living more of it and pursuing whatever freedom you choose along the way. I only know that freedom myself because I spent more than 30 years on the hamster wheel. A wheel I want to help you free yourself from forever.

This is Prohibited Profits.

CHAPTER 2

FINANCIAL RESET

I f you are like me, you probably grew up with a set of beliefs about money. I was told to follow the rules and get an education. Go to college, start my 401K, IRA, and open a savings account. If I was lucky I could retire at 65 to live comfortably for the rest of my life.

That model was set up for our parents and our grandparents before them. For their generation, the American dream may have been real. But what about your dreams? When you were growing up, did you dream about working at a job you hated for your entire life?

Intuitively, I knew there had to be a better path to freedom. I didn't want to spend my life struggling, away from my family like they did. That wasn't their fault either. They were programmed with scarce beliefs. The only way to survive was to work long, grueling hours at a job you didn't like. Eventually, you would be rewarded with a graceful retirement.

I know I didn't want that life. But even for me, I fell into that trap and spent most of my adult life working in corporate America. In the last chapter, I shared how I discovered Prohibited Profits. It's safe to say my parents were not pleased with my newfound wealth, or the way I was making it.

It was a straight path to military structure by way of the Marines. I excelled, it was made for me, I thrived in that militant environment. I found my voice, my confidence and my ability to lead through the Marines.

Eventually, I found myself working in corporate America, I was following the same blueprint I watched my parents follow.

I worked at Siemens medical for 15 years and I was secure. Securely trapped. It wasn't until I realized what I was trading for that freedom, that I really got serious about my future. My position had locked me in golden handcuffs.

I was making a solid 6-figure salary, and my investment accounts were on track. I was in the financial markets making 10-12% returns. My retirement accounts were growing, and I was on path to live comfortably once I retired.

Like many others, I was trading my freedom for that perception of "retirement." I was missing my life right now and trading it for a paycheck. My 2 kids were growing up and I found myself on the road 40 weeks per year. I will never forget the pain of telling my young children "good-night" on the phone from the other side of the country.

To this day, I wish I would have bet on myself sooner. I always trusted myself and my ability to get results, but I was afraid. I was afraid to leave and fail. I was afraid of the unknown. Deep down, I had doubts that I could find a better way. I wasn't in position to start my own medical company. Medical sales was what I knew.

While I trusted myself, didn't have the confidence to go all in. I didn't create enough certainty to go for it. The difference between who I was and who I became, was the certainty to take action. It was always "I'm working towards a better life." Instead of, "I'm taking action on my better life now."

If you are like me, you might be dealing with similar thoughts or justifications for why you are working that job you hate. Maybe you are reading this saying, "Seth, I like my job." I actually did too. If you like your job, and you are satisfied with current situation, you likely wouldn't be reading this book.

If you are open to being honest with yourself, ask yourself if you are truly fulfilled. Deep down, are there things you wish you could be doing? Are there things that you can't do because of your job or current financial situation? If that answer is yes, then congratulations, you have already started to think like a Prohibited Profits investor. The first step is to get mad at your current situation and make changes now, not later.

My decision was to figure out a way to provide for my family. Most importantly, I had to create a legacy and have time freedom to do what my parents couldn't. Once you make that decision, it's time to do the math and look at the truth about those secure retirement accounts.

Let's say you have a 401K, you've started an investment account, chased trends, hired mentors, hit consistent growth and diversified your portfolio, yet still feel like you are missing the biggest opportunities in the marketplace.

Maybe you've hit the average 10-12% stock market gains but still feel like you are not on path to reaching generational financial freedom.

There are an abundance of financial advisors and investment gurus in the marketplace that are government regulated to give you specific answers.

Maybe you have money to invest, but don't have the time to do the research to find the right opportunities with the most upside. There is over $15 trillion in the stock market and most of those opportunities are limited in upside.

The opportunities that can provide financial freedom, are not always available to the average person. Even the savviest financial advisor is programmed with their own set of limiting beliefs and impulse responses. They are there to make sure you don't lose your money, instead of chasing Prohibited Profits.

If 401K's, IRA's and traditional 10-12% returns were a sure thing, then it would make sense why some people choose that route. But what happens when the 2008 financial crisis wipes out more than 20% of your retirement accounts overnight? If you were nearing age 65, that would have setback the retirement you had been working 45 years to enjoy.

Even the most secure, conservative investments come with a gamble. Again in 2020, we saw another financial crisis plummet markets quickly. The market has come back faster and stronger than ever, but at what cost?

As of writing the book, the government is deeper in debt than at any time in our lives. Growing by the billions and yes, trillions. Speaking of Trillions. The U.S. government also decided to print trillions of dollars to save big business. Only a small part of that money went to the American people.

Anybody that understands how money works, knows that the money given to 99% of people, will eventually flow right back to the 1%. The average American has rent payments and homes owned by the wealthy. They pay for inflationary goods and have poor spending habits. There is a reason Best Buy ran out of 4K televisions when the American people got their stimulus packages.

The federal reserve is broken, out of hand and heading for disaster. Have you stopped to think about where those trillions of dollars are coming from? How they were created? If you asked for a loan, they would expect you to pay it back. However, the government seemingly never has to pay back their loans. We could be headed for a financial disaster where the U.S. dollar holds very little value.

We are all familiar with bail-outs. But what happens if a government faces its own crisis and they need money? That might sound crazy, but it happened in Cyprus. Cyprus had a bail-in and decided to save themselves instead of their citizens.

I am not suggesting that will happen in America, or any of the other large established countries. However, don't be blinded by the headlines about the strong economy and the solvency of the American dollar. We are more than 28 Trillion dollars in debt and eventually, someone is going to pay that debt.

More importantly for you, perhaps, what will be the value of your retirement account once you reach the age of 65? If you look at your retirement accounts, you may see projections of a few million dollars. You might be thinking "I can live comfortably with $1.6 million dollars when I retire."

Those current numbers feel safe. But what might happen when the cost of goods is 4X higher by the time you reach retirement? That $1.6 million might feel more like

$400,000 or less. Good luck living the rest of your life on $400,000.

That is the cold hard truth for many Americans. Once they reach retirement, their biggest fear becomes outliving their retirement. Imagine reaching the end of your life and thinking "I can't afford to stay alive." That is a real fear and the truth for many retirees.

I'm not sharing this information to scare you or to present a doomsday scenario. In fact, I'm suggesting the opposite.

If you are open to a new perspective and you can shift your own limiting beliefs. We are currently living through the biggest financial shift during our lifetime. A rare opportunity to create generational wealth for you and your family.

What if I told you that you could take advantage of these opportunities, while mitigating your own risk? What if I could show you a way to break free from the shackles of the American dream? There is a path to make money beyond your wildest imagination and have the freedom to watch your kids grow up.

You might have a job, 401K, retirement accounts that are working and a solid financial plan for the future.

If you are open to a new perspective, I am suggesting that you should pursue more 1000%+ upside opportunities. My goal is to open your eyes to these rare financial shifts.

Today, the everyday person has real opportunities to enter the 1%.

I lived through the dot com bubble, the real estate bubble and noticed the trends each time. A lot of people are afraid of the word bubble, because everyone knows bubbles can burst.

Most of us saw the horror stories. We listened to people tell us how they lost everything because they were overleveraged in real estate. However, most of the people that understand real estate, made millions again.

As an investor, I look at a bubble as an opportunity. Once you can get beyond the media, there are other stories of people who made multi-millions during that real estate bubble. They learned how the systems worked and they are doing it again now.

I watched investors make millions and billions during the recent cannabis prohibition era. These trends happen over and over and over if you will pay attention with your mind, instead of your eyes.

Again, not everyone will see these opportunities. That's what Prohibited Profits is all about. If it was a sure thing right now, everyone would be investing. By the time an investment has become a sure thing, it's no longer an opportunity. Once banks and hedge funds get involved, the opportunity becomes limited.

There is a reason you don't see overnight oil and commodities millionaires. Those markets are stable and are being traded by the biggest companies in the world. There is a reason people are not mining for gold like they did during the gold rush.

There is also a reason why legacies and fortunes are still enjoyed generations later. Gold rush and oil billionaires are still celebrated by their families because they got there first.

I had been watching all of the markets for years. I became fascinated with investments. I was trading commodities and futures on the side while working my corporate job. In 2015, all of this started to make sense for me. I saw the writing on the wall of where the American dollar was headed.

Knowledge isn't power, it's the potential for power. Unless you make a move, then you will always be the person saying, "what if." You probably know a lot of people like that.

I knew that if I was going to see my kids grow up, my intentions wouldn't cut it. I had to make a decision and take action. It was time for me to get real, raw and relevant with myself. I had to take control of my life.

Once I made that decision my perspective shifted. I was now looking for ways to make my decision a reality and nothing was going to stand in my way.

I noticed the trend coming with Bitcoin. Although it sounds like a safe bet today, Bitcoin was far from it in 2015. All of the financial principles I had learned my entire life added up. A universal currency that was finite that would eventually be accepted everywhere. If the American government continued to print money, their people would need to look elsewhere to protect their financial future.

For me, it wasn't IF Bitcoin would become mainstream. It was a question of WHEN. That is the risk of Prohibited Profits today with Bitcoin and Cryptocurrency. I knew it would take some time before the government would validate it. They have a lot to lose if Bitcoin succeeds. But I had 25+ years before I could cash in on my retirement accounts anyways.

I wasn't going to wait until I was old to enjoy my life or my money. It was time to be bold. I cashed out my 401K and all of my retirement accounts to invest in Bitcoin at $250.

Banks are starting to accept Bitcoin. Tesla carries Bitcoin on their balance sheet. The biggest funds in the world are buying Bitcoin. The Prohibited Profits opportunity on Bitcoin is still alive and well.

But it's time to look for the next opportunity, the next Bitcoin, whether that's in crypto or the next opportunity.

Prohibited Profits isn't about one specific opportunity. Prohibited Profits is about locating these 1000%+ opportunities years before they go mainstream. Prohibited Profits is about understanding modern shifts in wealth, especially when you can take advantage of them.

Today, you have access to these opportunities and can take advantage of them. The technology around blockchain technology is the biggest shift of our generation. We are living through the biggest economic shift of our lives. This is bigger than the dot.com boom if you know how to play the game.

This is your oil and gold rush opportunity. This is your opportunity to create that wealth for your family and for generations to come. The world has changed and now you have access like never before.

The question is, will you think about it? Or will you make the decision to go for it and change the trajectory of your life forever?

I know what you are thinking, "Seth that's pretty bold, I'm not putting my entire retirement and savings into speculation."

If that is what you are thinking, then I agree. But what if you started with 5% of your portfolio instead of 0%? What if you decided that you would be open to these high upside opportunities? What if you tested it instead of saying no?

Start with what you are willing to lose. Sure, every investment comes with some risk. You have likely heard the horror stories of people who were ripped off or lost money in crypto. You can also find thousands of those stories in the stock market as well. Investing carries speculative risk, no matter what you are investing in.

You can decide to test and learn for yourself. That might cost you money and time. You could also find a coach or mentor that understands the markets.

I often hear people say, "I want to invest in ____ but I don't want to pay a coach because that's money I could have invested in _____."

Prohibited Profits come with a time vs opportunity cost. Let's say you had $5000 to invest. You could invest that $5000 into an asset, watch, learn and see what happens. However, what if you invested $1000 into your education? Or into a coach that has proven results? Your $4000 remaining balance will outperform the $5000 novice every time.

Here is another example on the importance of time. Do the math. What if I would have had a great or advisor telling me about Bitcoin in 2009 instead of 2015? In 2009, Bitcoin was trading at .06 cents. When I invested in 2015, it was around $225. If I paid for the knowledge in 2009, I could have invested $100 and been set for life.

The opportunity and the timing matters more than the investment. If you can pay for an education or partner with someone that will help you put your money in the right place, you can create more wealth, faster.

The phrase "time is money" has never been more money. Every day you wait, you are paying a waiting tax on your future life. Every Prohibited Profits opportunity requires certainty and a quick decision. Will you take advantage of the opportunities while they are here? Or will you continue to speculate, and watch others get ahead?

100 years from now, we will still be talking about the financial legacies being created right now. They will either be talking about you, or the people you will come to know. The great thing about Prohibited Profits is that once you make a decision and decide to go all in, it doesn't have to take forever to change your life.

The goal of this book is to open your eyes to the opportunities in front of you right now. It's also to help you spot these trends so that you can take advantage of these opportunities in the future.

My goal is to help you wake up to the myth of a secure retirement and encourage you to look for life changing opportunities, no matter what they look like. In the next chapter, I will share with you my process, to locate 1000% upside opportunities. I will also share how you can take advantage of them and ultimately keep more money in your pocket.

Prohibited Profits is about taking advantage of those opportunities and keeping more of your hard-earned money.

The first step to changing your financial future and guaranteeing your families future is to make a decision. Are you committed to securing your piece of the Prohibited Profits?

CHAPTER 3

PROFITS PROCESS

Prohibited Profits is about the opportunity, not simply the vehicle. Most of us are looking at opportunities only in mainstream emerging trends. We want to follow the crowd because we see other people generating wealth. If you look around you, wherever you are right now, you can likely spot wealth everywhere. People made millions because of real estate, construction, and automobiles.

Everything from the coffee we drink, to the water bottles we buy and the pet food we purchase for our animals. For someone out there, these were Prohibited Profit opportunities. Yet many of us are stuck in the frame. We can't see those opportunities because we tend to get caught with our blinders on.

It is easy to get stuck in our day to day life and forget about all of these opportunities. Right now, everyone is chasing the real estate and Bitcoin gold rush, and rightfully so. In a future chapter, I will share my investment model. I will also share my 11-point system for investing in new crypto technology.

But again, this isn't just a book about Bitcoin or Blockchain. This is about looking for these opportunities everywhere. It's about becoming a magnet for opportunities instead of limiting your success.

Let me share a quick story to set the framework and open your mind to all of the possibilities in the world. I remember last summer, taking my youngest 2 kids out to our property in Colorado. A month-long summer bonding trip I didn't get to take with my oldest children when they were younger. It was a beautiful reminder of my why. We spent time exploring the mountains and seeing national parks.

Then for a few days, we decided to plant pistachio seeds. An entire farm of pistachio seeds. Part of the reason for our 2-week trip, was to build something. I wanted to create an asset that would pay them compounded wealth forever.

It takes a lot of discipline to invest in a tree farm or a pistachio farm, but I have done both. The reason I share this with you, is because I see the short-term mindset taking over the marketplace right now. Everyone is chasing fast money, hoping to get their piece of the pie. But if you're only investment is in cryptocurrency, you are exposed.

Yes, the guy that runs a crypto hedge fund is telling you to diversify your portfolio. As soon as the opportunity in crypto has vanished, I will be in the next Prohibited Profits market. I share that because that's how I think about investing. I look at risks and measure against upside potential. If you do the math on a pistachio farm, the only costs associated are the land, the seeds and a little maintenance.

Unlike crypto, it will take me decades so see a profit from that work and of course there is risk. But there is also more than 1000% return upside. 1000% returns are the first thing I look for when investing in an opportunity. Why? Because I don't want to wait until I'm 65 to enjoy my life. I also understand the power of compound interest.

"Those that understand compound interest, earn it. While those who don't, pay it."

My life changed the day I was sitting in a classroom and my teacher shared this simple lesson I will never forget. In reality, it's one of the few things the education system delivered for me.

"Would you rather have $1 Million cash, or would you rather double a penny every day for 30 days?"

The question seemed simple enough. Give me the million in cash, please and thank you.

"If I give you a penny at the beginning of the month and double it every day, how much will you have by the end of the month."

Sounds simple enough. How could a penny be worth anything? But then we started to do the math.

Day 1 .01 X .01 = 2 pennies

Day 2 .02 X .02 = 4 pennies

I will save you the math lesson and get to the punchline. At the start, the numbers are insignificant.

But by day 27 the numbers look a little different. Now there is $671,088.64 and by day 30, that number has risen to $5,368,709.12.

I definitely would have regret taking the $1 million even at that age. Why am I sharing this part of the story? Because the Prohibited Profits method is a 3-step approach that's starts with locating 1000% upside opportunities.

Why 1000%?

Remember, we want to find rare upside opportunities before the masses. Just like finding gold during the gold rush, we want to be heavily rewarded for our investment. 1000% upside allows you to pull profits, then re-invest into the next 1000% opportunity.

Before I share my 3-step process to create your own Prohibited Profits, I want to share a few other principles that will help you along your financial journey.

Principle # 1: Invest In Solving Problems- When you think about investing, start by looking at technology that solves big problems. There is a reason that Tesla, Uber and Bitcoin were all such great investments. They solve significant problems for the world. Each company provided far better solutions than their predecessors.

Principle #2: Cost vs Price- Earlier, I shared this principle in depth with the example of a $5000 investor. In almost all cases, there will be an education tax for those getting started. If you choose to experiment over hiring a coach, you will pay for your education.

The education might be a significant investment, but the cost far outweighs the price. Imagine if you hired a coach in 2009 that told you to invest $100 into Bitcoin.

You would be a billionaire and no matter what their fee is, it would have been worth it. Consider the opportunity cost of missing opportunities. Opportunity cost is more expensive than the price of mentorship and education. In the game of Prohibited Profits, there is always a waiting tax for those who want to learn the hard way.

Principle #3: Look for trends before they go mainstream- If you are in the crypto markets currently, you understand the opportunity still available for you. But even Bitcoin and crypto have a Prohibited Profits expiration date. Remember, your profit when Bitcoin went from $1 to $2 is the same as rising from $50,0000 to $100,000.

Now that Bitcoin has hit the mainstream, the Prohibited Profits opportunity is in the next coin that solves problems. I am also looking the future of psilocybin and other future technology. You want to be the first to know, instead of the last.

Let's talk about the importance of first movers advantage. The person who struck oil first, made the most money. The person who reached the goldmine first, made the most money. However, they also took the most risk. Fortune rewards those who are bold and chase what they want. If there is a security blanket and the investment is "safe," there is no upside. There will be sharks in the water buying.

My current favorite path to apply first movers advantage is through cryptocurrency. Although, Bitcoin has gone mainstream. the rest of the blockchain and crypto game is still being speculated by the masses. There is a window to take advantage of the opportunity and if you see the world like I do. Bitcoin is my main currency and will be for the foreseeable future.

Each time I lock in profits from another investment, I convert that investment back into Bitcoin. I truly believe in the future and compound effect of Bitcoins growth. I will bet on Bitcoin over the microscopic earnings most people receive from savings accounts and low yield bonds.

5 years ago, I started "Crypto Wealth Coach," and created my 11-point checklist for anything myself or my students invest in. I am not in the casino to gamble. I have been

investing in commodities and futures markets for 20+ years. I live by the Warren Buffet rule of investing.

Rule #1 "Don't lose my money"

Rule #2 "See rule #1"

This is my life because making money can be the easy part once you know what to look for. Once you understand the Prohibited Profits checklist, you will become an opportunity magnet. However, it's not always what you make, it's what you can keep and ultimately compound.

STEP 1: LOCATING OPPORTUNITIES

Every investment I make starts with this foundational principle. As an investor, my focus is on creating as many compound interest opportunities that I can. That might mean a pistachio farm that yields 1000%+ upside. Do I always wait until my investment reaches 1000%? Almost never. Later in this book, I will share my full exit strategy. I will teach you how to pull back profits so that you reduce risks and "let it ride" with upside advantage.

As an investor, it's our job to turn investments into profits. I see so many investors touting their earnings and gains. But until you sell a position and lock in profits, those are only potential profits.

Every investment we look for at least 100% return on our initial investment. That means, if I am investing $100,000 into a tree farm, I better make at least a $200,000 profit or it was a failed investment.

Once an investment hits 300%, I will start to pull back profits to cover the initial investment. At that point, you can leave the rest in without risk. You have tripled your original investment and can compound those profits without exposure.

What do you do with your initial investment? Put it back into a Prohibited Profits opportunity and repeat that cycle over and over again. In future chapters, we will discuss the other points on my investment checklist. For now, I want you to be aware of what to look for and how to hunt for these opportunities.

What do you do with your initial investment? Put it back into a Prohibited Profits opportunity and repeat that cycle over and over again. In future chapters, we will discuss the other points on my investment checklist. For now, I want you to be aware of what to look for and how to hunt for these opportunities.

For me, Investing is my life.

STEP 2: TAKING ACTION

"I had the idea for Uber years before Uber even existed"

I'm sure you have heard a quote like this around your local watercooler. The shoulda, coulda, woulda, has-beens are everywhere. They are quick to tell you about what they could have done or what they knew to be true.

When I was working in corporate America, I deep down knew there had to be a better way to earn a living and live my life. I knew there had to be a better way, but for many years I stayed stuck at my job. Maybe you are in a situation that you don't like right now. Perhaps you know a better life is out there and that you are capable of achieving your dreams.

The best of intentions lay in the graveyard, because intentions don't get results. Action gets results.

At the writing of this book, I have created more than 50+ millionaires through my coaching programs. However, there have been hundreds of people still watching from the sidelines. They have seen our predicted investments go up 1000%+. But they still say they are waiting on the right opportunity.

Taking action sounds simple. But taking action is the most difficult step that most of us don't integrate. It's one thing to say, "I am an action taker." It's another to buy a ticket to the game and put your chips on the table.

Did you know that over 80% of diet supplements never get opened? There is a real problem in our world currently and most of it is tied to the identity of what we intend to do, NOT what we do.

It was bold for me to tout Bitcoin as the next big investment opportunity when it was at $225. Had I told some of my friends, they might have pat me on the back and said, "great call Seth." But pats on the back don't pay the bills and all of your woulda, couldas won't help either.

Investing and life is about what you actually do, not what you say you are going to do. Make the commitment to be golden to your word. Decide to take action that matches your level of risk tolerance.

I am not suggesting that you have to cash out your 401K and retirement funds to chase the next big thing. But I am saying to put your chips on the table. What can you afford to invest? If it's $1000 then start there. If it's $5000, do that. But don't sit on the sideline forever waiting for the right time.

"The best time to plant a tree was 20 years ago. The next best time is right now."

STEP 3: KEEPING YOUR MONEY

Most investors want to talk about their topline revenue and for good reason. Of course, revenue is important. However, if you don't understand how to keep more of your hard-earned money, then you still don't understand Prohibited Profits. Once you understand compound interest, you will start to look at taxes and savings differently.

$100 may not sound like a lot of money but remember our "double a penny" strategy. I view every dollar as a million-dollar opportunity, because in this game, it is.

Here's the disclaimer. YOU HAVE TO PAY YOUR TAXES! IF YOU DON'T PAY YOUR TAXES THEY WILL THROW YOU IN JAIL.

Now that we have covered that, let's talk about how you can pay less in taxes and keep more of that money. The reason they don't teach taxes and government loopholes in school is because knowledge is power. If the people don't know that these legalities exist, then the government gets to keep more of your money.

Say what you want about Donald Trump, but when his taxes came out, I was not surprised one bit to see how little he had paid. Donald Trump is a smart and savvy business-man when it comes to tax law. Anyone saying differently, is fighting for a system that isn't fighting for you.

Let me repeat that, why would you EVER fight for a government who is hoping you pay them more of the money you work hard for? Especially when they created the rules, laws and loopholes that the ultra-wealthy know and leverage.

Keeping more of your money should be applauded. It means you are educating yourself on the rules of money. In future chapters, I will share some of these exact strategies that you can apply in your own life to keep more of your money.

Establishing international residencies or citizenship and investing into real estate comes with huge tax breaks. These breaks will help you invest more of your money into yourself and your family instead of the U.S. Government.

Prohibited Profits is about taking control of your life at every level. Many people are asleep at the wheel. They are waiting for somebody else to tell them about the right opportunity. They are always waiting for the next big thing and they think the government is here to protect their wealth.

When you decide to take the leap into Prohibited Profits, you are accepting responsibility for everything. You accept responsibility for understanding your investment opportunities. You are responsible for taking action with your money. You also take accountability for learning (or hiring) the right people to help you keep more of your money.

Most people simply don't want that responsibility. They would rather have the symbol of safety and a secure retirement at the end of their lives. It is a lot of work to keep up with new technology. It takes a lot of certainty to make big investments. The government definitely doesn't make it easy to keep up with their tax codes.

We are not in this for easy. Prohibited Profits means accepting full responsibility. Take control of every area of your finances and your life. As you will see in the next chapter, getting started is almost always the most difficult part.

CHAPTER 4

BEGINNERS SWITCH-UP

If you decide to take advice from someone, make sure they have reached the goals that you are hoping to achieve. If I wanted to learn how to play basketball, I would probably take advice from someone like Lebron James. If I wanted to learn how to fix my car, I would take advice from an auto-mechanic.

A big problem we face, is that we tend to take advice from people that love us. We think that because they love and care about us, they are probably giving us sound advice. Oftentimes, those people are our parents, siblings, grandparents and closest friends. Just because they care about you, doesn't mean they are giving you quality advice.

I would argue that it's the opposite sometimes. The people closest to you will often share advice that will keep you safe.

Entrepreneurship and risk taking is difficult. Those people you love, likely were not entrepreneurs themselves. For

41

them, doing something new and taking risks is scary or seems impossible. Those are limitations they put on themselves a long time ago.

Although they may love you, you likely realize that they gave up on their dreams a long time ago. They decided to go the safe route and they are programmed to help you play it safe too. That is not their fault. They have been programmed their entire life to rely on the system that I hope you want to break free from.

Remember, it's not your loved ones fault that they want to protect you. But it is your decision to take their advice and kill your own dreams. That's why the phrase "you are the sum of the 5 people you spend the most time with."

As a child, you don't always get to make that choice. Many of you may have had similar childhoods as me, where I had very little support at home. Some of you may have grown up comfortably and middle class. Perhaps you did grow up around wealth and that shaped the beliefs you have today.

No matter what your circumstance is, ask yourself what you really want out of life. Then ask who has achieved those goals. If you are comfortable working 40 years of your life, then take advice from someone who has. If you want to retire with $500,000 to live out the rest of your days, then take advice from someone who has achieved that. They will probably have great advice on how to manage relationships and how to be a great employee.

If you want to live a different life, make sure to take your advice from people that have done it. The best way is to learn from people that are currently doing it. There are ultra-successful millionaires that I also wouldn't take advice from.

Why? Because many of them are sitting on their success from years ago and are not playing the game anymore. They may be able to share how they had success, and you can draw great lessons from their story. But this is your future, not theirs. Ask yourself if their advice is relevant to the life you want to live.

Remember, you are making a decision to take control over everything in your life. That means taking advice and spending time with people who are living it. Spend time around people building their Prohibited Profits right now. The world moves too fast and what worked yesterday, won't work today or tomorrow. Blockbuster and taxicab companies are great examples.

Sure, there are millionaire CEO's from Blockbuster. I bet there is a taxicab fleet owner that cashed out just in time. Your mind can and will always shift to the future once you adopt the Prohibited Profits mindset. It's not about what you have done. This is about the relevant, current and future success you are building for your own family.

Getting started is always the most difficult part. The vision seems too far away and feels out of reach for you. You might be reading this thinking "I see people making millions in crypto, but that will never be me."

LIMITATIONS & MYTHS

We tend to put limitations on ourselves because all that we know, is our current life and memories from the past. But there are thousands of lessons of people that went from rags to riches. There are plenty of normal people like me who said that enough is enough and committed to a new life. You might not ever start if you don't think you are capable of reaching your goals.

Start by looking at your own limitations about what is possible for you. Most people overestimate what they can do in 1 year, but far underestimate what they can do in 5 years.

Once you get clear on what you want, create a belief that you can actually achieve it. Creating belief starts by taking action and writing a new story for your mind. Once you see it's possible, commit to figuring it out instead of saying "oh I could never…"

Learned helplessness is a very real circumstance in our society. The myth of financial freedom has been taught to us for years. Many people don't want to hunt for success or take responsibility for their lives. They would rather wait around for that secure retirement at the end of the rainbow of life. That or the stimulus check fairy that will save the day.

I was caught in the same trap when I realized that nobody was coming to save me. I had to figure it out for myself and create my own financial future.

At this point, you likely have a secure path or perhaps a plan for your financial future. If you currently have a 401K, you understand the importance of saving money. Perhaps Robinhood got you with their free stock campaigns. At least you have started to think about your financial future.

You might even be putting some money in the game of crypto. Maybe Elon Musk got you with his dog memes and you are planning your trip to Mars as we speak. I share these examples because that represents a lot of people in the investing market right now. Many people are dabbling and making moves to find hope for a better tomorrow.

These are great intentions, but really it is more wheel spinning. Most people are interested in their financial future, but are they 100% committed?

If you picked up this book, you are taking the right step in the direction with your actions. But no matter how many times you check that 401K account, it's not going to shift your financial future.

I remember being in the same situation. Staring at my investment accounts, justifying every decision I was making.

Then one day I got angry. It was time for me to cut the bullshit and get out of the story I was telling myself. I told myself a story that I would get that raise and make enough money to live comfortably. I didn't want comfortable! Growing up, I had big ambitions to build a dynasty for my family.

Maybe you had similar dreams? But then life got in the way and you told yourself why you couldn't achieve those dreams.

It takes courage to get real, raw and relevant with yourself. Ask yourself "is this the dream I had for my life?" That was a difficult moment for me, to break down and get honest with myself about where I was in my life. I reminded myself that I was actually being a bad father and husband, even though I told myself I was doing everything for them.

I hope you can have that real, raw and urgent moment for yourself too. Once you do, everything can change for the better.

Start from wherever you are now and make the decision to change your life forever, one step and one day at a time. Course correct back to that dream and make the decision to go for it. Now, let's get tactical.

Start with knowledge, mentorship & audit your circle

Once I decided to change my life, I knew I had to commit to personal growth. I invested in every relevant book I could find. I hired coaches and joined multiple

46

Masterminds. I had some coaches for finance and others for personal development.

Working with a financial coach will help you cut down on your investing learning curve. But if you can't learn to get out of your own way, eventually you will fail. Investing is a forever game and requires discipline that most people cannot sustain.

You have probably heard the horror stories or seen the type in movies. Losing sleep over losses, glued to their computer 20 hours per day and drinking enough coffee to support a small village.

My goal was to be a better husband and father, not a more distant one. I wanted more personal freedom, not a financial prison. So it was up to me to learn how to control my emotions and my mind when things got hot. Anyone thinking about investing should think about this concept called "manageable cadence."

Manageable cadence is a concept that will help you avoid burnout. Ask yourself, what can I do every day, with consistency, that will compound my results for the better? I created an entire process with notifications, alerts and buy/sell signals for my investments.

Sure, there may be the rare occasion where I wake up at 3 AM to make a trade. But for the most part, think about designing a sustainable life for yourself. For me, that meant investing into coaching and mentorship.

Next, audit your circle of friends and the people you spend the most time with. Are they going in the same direction as you? Do they also share your big goals and aspirations? People will either push you to become the best you can be, or they will try to pull them back to where they are.

Consider auditing the people you spend the most time with. Ask yourself if they are fueling or stunting your growth. That doesn't mean you should stop talking to your best friend or leave your parents behind. Being aware of the people who are pushing or pulling you, gives you the freedom to protect your own energy. You can still spend time with them, but don't allow them to influence the decisions you have made in your life.

Finally, find mentorship from people that you do want to be like. That was masterminds, events and coaches for me. I understood the importance of proximity and being around likeminded people. If you are struggling with self-belief about what is possible, then get around people that have already achieved success.

One, you will realize that many of them are very human. No matter a person's success, we all have our flaws, struggles and challenges in life. By joining masterminds, It was easy to see that success was attainable. The ultra-successful people were not extraordinary. They were just extra-focused on their outcomes and driven towards success.

Masterminds and events also give you the chance to open your mind to other Prohibited Profits opportunities. If you are feeling stuck, it's likely because you are too close to your current situation. As one of my coaches always says, "You can't see the picture when you are standing in the frame."

It's essential to always be adjusting our perspective to what is possible. Also ask yourself, what is currently relevant? While my mind is on cryptocurrency, I may be missing a new technology breakthrough. By going to a mastermind, I might find an opportunity that someone else has discovered. When we realize that we don't know what we don't know, we can always be curious. Curiosity will help you find future Prohibited Profits opportunities.

Some of you might be thinking, "I would love to do all of that, but I don't have the money yet."

I have been there too. One of my first mentors was Warren Buffett. No I haven't met Warren Buffet, but he was an early financial mentor for me. Your mentors don't have to be someone you know, as long as they are living the life you want to live. Find mentorship in books, podcasts, audiobooks, YouTube videos and follow people that inspire you. Don't just listen to what they say, watch what they do. Actions always speak louder than words.

The greatest athletes and entrepreneurs in the world have multiple coaches and mentors. As I mentioned in the first chapter, I always suggest investing into coaches and mentorship if you have the money. They will save you time and the opportunity cost of self-educating.

Finally, if you are just getting started, take one small action to start building momentum. The first step is the hardest step. Once you do start, you will learn exponentially faster because now you have skin in the game.

Make your first investment, go to your first event or subscribe to a podcast if that's what it takes. Start where you can. Commit to compounding knowledge, relationships and taking little steps in a new direction. Maybe that first step feels like it's only worth a penny but imagine what you can do in 30 days.

CHAPTER 5

INVESTORS GAME-CHANGER

If you have already started investing, you have already committed to more action that most Americans. When I say investing, that means beyond the 401K and standard savings plan. If you have opened a Robin Hood account or started a Coinbase account, congratulate yourself on taking the initiative to invest into your future.

Many people who decide to jump into investing are still looking for that quick fix approach.

"Seth, will you just send me your picks?"

I was the same way once. I will never forget investing into one of my first mastermind groups after deciding to turn trading into my full-time profession. At that time, cannabis was the Prohibited Profits opportunity and I was looking for my slice of the pie. I recall asking for candlestick charts and picks.

One of my personal mentors, Jaramy Eugene Wilson, shared a valuable lesson that I would like to share with you. He said "if you are looking for picks, you are in the wrong place. We teach people the principles of investing and the strategy behind each of these picks. Otherwise, if I just sent picks, you might not know the reasoning behind it. You might look at that information a day late and our position has changed."

It was exactly how I thought about investing and it made perfect sense. Perhaps you are in the same position right now. You are committed to investing into your future, but not committed to learning the game. Commit to learning the foundation of why an opportunity is "investible."

I will dive into my 11-point checklist for investing in chapter 7. However, I want you to understand the importance of understanding your craft. Don't chase stock tips. If you are not willing to educate yourself, you will dilute yourself and could end up losing all of your money.

As of right now, there are over 10,000 different cryptocurrencies and growing. That's not considering stock markets, futures or commodities markets I trade in as well.

If you are serious about investing, it's important to understand that this is a lifestyle. Investing is not gambling or a get rich quick scheme. I spend full days, weeks and often months doing research on companies. I want to know everything before I ever invest my money.

Most people end up diluting themselves and their initial investment. Instead of doing the research to find the true winning opportunities, they put "some" money into 5 different investments. They are gambling like a roulette wheel, hoping one hits. They are chasing every opportunity that seems trendy and making emotional decisions based on FOMO (fear of missing out).

When you chase 5 rabbits, you catch none.

At least you are chasing the rabbits while others are watching them run. Don't feel ashamed or guilty for chasing each opportunity. You are taking action and realize the opportunity available to people right now.

Have you ever fallen into this trap? Looking for stock picks on social media? Listening to people with no track record tout winners? Watching YouTube videos of people that are inexperienced and underqualified. In fact, 98% of all people fall into this trap at least once when they start investing.

You might even be thinking to yourself, "But it's working Seth, I'm making my 12% yearly returns and building my portfolio."

The problem with dilution isn't that you won't create some success. You likely could diversify enough to get some returns. But you are not hyper-focused on creating 100%+ returns. Instead of investing into 5 different opportunities, where 3 might lose and 2 might win. What if you had a system that created so much certainty that you only needed to invest into that 1 winner?

Does that mean all of my picks are winners? Absolutely not. My losses are documented right beside my wins. But it does mean I have created a system that helps me pick more consistent winners. Most importantly, I capitalize on the upside of those winners and minimize losses on the losers.

Immediately, my 11-point checklist narrows the investing options down to .27% of those 10,000+ different opportunities.

As I shared earlier in the book, I was born and trained to be a Marine. I'm proud of it. It's tattooed on my body because of what the Marines did for me. It's a significant part of my story and who I am today.

I share that to frame a scenario. If we were going into battle in enemy territory, there are 2 options. We could run in like crazy people, spray and pray machine gun rounds. We could hope we hit our target and potentially get shot or killed in the process.

OR we could be strategic, create a plan, get laser focused on our target and create a clean shot from a sniper a mile away.

In scenario 1, we might have success, but there's also a chance that we die or hurt innocent people with crossfire.

In scenario 2, we execute a plan and hit our target safely without injuring others or ourselves.

For me, scenario 2 is always the best option. However, many people investing opt for scenario 1. They tell themselves they are "diversifying" and limiting their risk. In reality, they haven't done the research or invested into a process to create certainty.

Instead of being laser focused on one solid opportunity, they are shooting up the town, hoping that one hits. That one or two out of five might hit, but instead of having one big winner, they have a winner and 4 losses. Their portfolio might show green numbers. But they don't understand the opportunity cost of the inexperience tax they are paying.

OPPORTUNITY COST & INEXPERIENCE TAX

A few years ago a good friend of mine came to me with an opportunity in the cannabis industry. He was also trying to get out of the rat race and decided to go for it. Only he didn't know anything about the industry, he just knew it was a Prohibited Profits opportunity.

He decided to uproot his life and move to the west coast to chase this cannabis opportunity. He invested $400,000 to start his cannabis grow and distribution business and wanted me to invest as well. At the time, he asked me to invest $30,000 into his business. I could have invested in the opportunity and it would not have hurt me financially. Remember, I only invest when an opportunity meets my Prohibited Profits checklist.

This opportunity did not. Eventually it failed because my friend was inexperienced. He didn't realize that the cannabis market had been widely saturated. He was entering a market that had already passed the opportunity window. Similar to the oil industry, eventually the wells dry up. You don't want to be the person left holding the empty dry land.

He paid a high inexperience tax because he didn't understand the business he was getting into. He didn't know how difficult it would be to be successful. If he would have hired a consultant that knew the cannabis industry, he may have lost $20,000 to the consultant. I'd rather lose $20,000 instead of $400,000 all day.

His inexperience tax cost him more than $400,000. It cost him his freedom and future livelihood because he is back working long hours at a job he doesn't like. His inexperience tax didn't just cost money, it cost him his financial future.

Being able to say NO, is far more powerful than saying yes. Every day we are bombarded with ideas and opportunities. I have never met an investment where the person said, "this one is definitely a loser." Everyone is an optimist and believes their investment is the right one, until it's not.

When you say no, you are saying yes to a better opportunity. On the other hand, every time you say yes to an opportunity, you are saying no to something else.

Let's say I did invest into his cannabis business and my $30K investment turned into $60K. That would be a great investment, right? For most people, the answer would be a resounding yes and had I known that, I probably would have invested. But the opportunity cost is what I hope you understand most.

Instead of investing $30K into cannabis, I decided to invest it into Bitcoin. Now, that $30K is worth over $600,000. That was the opportunity cost of saying no to his cannabis opportunity. I was saying no to turning 30K into 60K. Instead, I was able to find a better Prohibited Profits opportunity to make $600K instead.

I share that example, not to brag, but to tie in a point that separates the average investor from someone who builds generational wealth. Chance favors the bold, they say. I agree, and it also rewards those who ask better questions and find the right opportunity.

There are winning opportunities everywhere in today's marketplace. But not every opportunity is created equal and you can't pursue everything.

If you wanted to become an expert carpenter, plumber or mechanic, you would hire an expert carpenter, plumber or mechanic. We all understand this when it comes to specialty trade. But investing is tricky because everyone has become an expert investor. As long as you have Facebook or Instagram, you can post your winners and look like an expert.

However, they don't understand a track record for proven results. They haven't been in the game for decades, trading at a high level. They don't realize that markets shift, and todays success does not predict future success.

Most people assume they can do it themselves, and many of them can in the short term. But if you are serious about creating life-changing wealth, it's probably worth it to hire an expert coach. Find someone who has a long-term track record.

You can only learn by investing and your first investment should always be into yourself. After you invest in yourself, then consider a coach who can take you to the next level. A coach will help you create certainty to see the right opportunities. Stop diluting your investments because of your risk uncertainty.

Before you invest any money into an opportunity. Ask yourself first if you are an expert. If you are not, then make sure you understand the inexperience tax and the opportunity cost of each decision.

ACCREDITED MYTHS

If you are an accredited investor or someone who has been trading for years, you might be resistant to some of the ideas in this book. Things are working for you right now, so why change?

You are investing and committed to your plan. You have buying into low risk/low upside opportunities and your portfolio is growing steadily. You might even be on the fast track to retirement and life is good. You understand how the markets work and you run a business of your own. You might not have the time to invest into understanding a new opportunity like crypto.

At this point, it's worth asking the question, are you in a fixed or growth mindset? If you are comfortable with where you are currently, you probably didn't buy this book. That or you stopped reading a long time ago. Even if you have millions saved for retirement, chances are you want more.

You deserve to be selfish with your financial future and your family's future. Also, make sure to consider your age and risk threshold. If you are 30 years old, you will likely be open to more risk than someone at age 63, for good reason.

No matter your age, I am inviting you to take more risks because you don't know the opportunities that you are missing by not chasing Prohibited Profits. If you are nearing retirement, holding millions, consider the risk of investing into crypto or the next opportunity.

Your $1 million could be on the trajectory for $40 million and a completely different future, instead of $1.1 million and a safety net.

There has never been a better opportunity than right now to chase Prohibited Profits. Remember, start with what you can afford to invest. Instead of sitting on your money in a savings account or 401K, what if you decided to allocate 1% of your wealth to taking more risks?

For the person at age 63, a 1% investment isn't going to wipe out their portfolio so close to retirement. For the person at age 30, I would argue they should be investing 90-100% of their wealth into the right opportunities.

No matter what your risk threshold it, it's time to consider more upside opportunities while they are available to the masses. If you are investing in crypto already, consider looking for the next technology that is emerging instead of sitting on Bitcoin. There is a limited opportunity right now to chase wealth beyond your wildest dreams.

Consider the opportunity cost of not going for it. Compare that to those extra 1% gains that won't make a difference once you retire anyways. Ask yourself where you can take more risks, without sacrificing your peace of mind. No matter where you are at in your investing life, I would encourage all of you to take on more calculated risks.

CHAPTER 6

WEALTH FORMULA

Conventional thinking got us into this situation in the first place. Most people are following the 401K and diversified investment model. This is what I like to call the "U.S. Dollar model." If you are banking on your 401K for your retirement, you are putting your future into a government that doesn't care about you. The government has far bigger issues to deal with than your retirement.

Up until now, this book has shared mindsets conversions and challenged beliefs about the future. It has also challenged you to take radical responsibility for your future. Instead of waiting for the government or someone else to bail you out, become your own hero. My hope is that this book will inspire you to act on the information and take control of your life.

If you take a step back and look at wealth from a 30,000-foot perspective, there are only 4 ways to build sustainable wealth. Of course, there are more than 4 ways to make money. But there are truly only 4 ways to builds wealth.

1. Build a business- If you are an entrepreneur, you can build a company that solves a real and relevant problem, you will acquire wealth. Most people must accumulate wealth in order to invest. It doesn't simply appear out of thin air and most of us don't have a trust fund or inheritance. Many successful investors started a business. Their business allowed them enough capital to fund their future investments.

2. Stocks & Bonds- This is everything under the investing category. The stock market has created more millionaires and billionaires than almost any other industry besides real estate. Some would argue that crypto would be in this category, but crypto is an asset in my opinion and hopefully yours too.

3. Assets- Real estate has produced more millionaires than any other category. If you can acquire assets in real estate, you will always build wealth. At least until we figure out flying cars or Elon puts us on Mars. Real estate isn't going anywhere, anytime soon. In a later chapter, I will also share some of the tax benefits of being in the crypto and real estate industry.

4. Commodities- These markets are great because they keep your money liquid. Oil, sugar, gold, copper and others. I can trade in and out of those markets very quickly. I prefer commodities over stocks for that reason.

THE WEALTH MATRIX

Now let's talk about how we make money. My favorite quote is "those that understand compound interest earn it while those that don't, pay it."

We live in a world of inflation. Every day prices are going up on everyday goods. I will talk about this more in a future chapter. It's important to understand how the wealthy leverages money to make more money. Whereas the middle-class trades time for money.

There are only 4 ways to make money. The first way is the most popular and widely accepted. You can be an employee. Employees trade time for money. Even if they make commissions, an employee's salary is capped because there are only 24 hours in a day. An employee will never outperform the people at higher levels.

Next is small businesses. These are your local gas stations, a bakery or an online store. Small businesses can be highly profitable into eight figures. But there is usually a reason they don't scale. Over 98% of businesses fail to scale past regional success.

Small business owners still trade time for money because they are running their small business. They might hire a manager, but they are the one that gets phone call when things go wrong. You still have to deal with headaches and employees. The small business is still trading time for money.

Big business includes businesses like Microsoft, Apple, Nike. These are some of the biggest businesses in the world. They have big corporations and hundreds if not thousands of employees. The CEO gets paid based on company performance. At this level, at least you have leverage to grow your income. That's why some CEO's are making $30 Million per year.

They want to leverage other people's time to increase their profits. 100 people at 10% output will always outperform you at 100% output. If you can grow to 100 employees, you have more leverage working for you.

Next is the investor. The investor is leveraging other companies to make money for them. Whether it's lumber, real estate, or the stock exchange, they look for opportunities to leverage money and make more money. If you can learn this art, you can buy back your time and head on a path towards financial freedom.

Finally, there's the last level. The private island, build your own space company type of wealth. That is one that I am still pursuing myself.

MYTH OF DIVERSIFICATION

Once you narrow it down to those four things, you can get clear on a strategy. There is a myth that you should diversify everything. A fun buzz word you hear, "make sure you diversify your portfolio," your expert uncle might say. Many people end up diversifying until there's no more money to be made.

They put 5% here, 5% there and eventually you have 20 positions that can't or won't make them rich. Sure, maybe you make 20-30% returns, but this is about upside potential and minimizing risk. Instead, invest into a Prohibited Profits opportunity like crypto. Now, you are chasing these 1000% upside opportunities.

Some may see it as "riskier", but the point of investing is to get wealthy. I am an investor, not a gambler remembers. There is less risk because my 11-point checklist that creates winning investments. I make every trade that I recommend to my groups.

Your financial advisor is legally bound to tell you about 401K's and conservative options. But are they trying to make you wealthy or keep their commissions coming in? How invested are they into making sure you reach financial freedom?

I know my level of commitment, because my family's livelihood and future are invested with each of the decisions I make. For that reason, I spend weeks or months researching companies. I speak with leadership teams, dissect white papers and understand everything about an opportunity before investing. This is the opportunity of a lifetime, and it can't be left to chance.

For that reason, I created this 11-point checklist so that I didn't have to "diversify" everything down to dilution. When you take bold action, you get bold results. That doesn't mean every investment is a winning opportunity. But it does mean that I invest confidently knowing the track record of my checklist.

GROWTH OR SCARCITY MINDSET?

Hello Dave Ramsey,

Nobody ever got wealthy because they stopped buying Starbucks.

You can't save your way to wealth; you must earn it. Sure, the extra $100 per month from Starbucks might make a difference over 50 years. But is that really how you want to live your life? Questioning every little decision in exchange for happiness 30 years from now?

Life is about decisions and I don't think that one sounds great. Instead, think of ways you can expand and increase your income. I want you to think big, so that you can start investing in Prohibited Profits opportunities. Your goal should be to buy a Starbucks franchise, instead of skipping out on $3 coffee.

Start thinking bigger about your life. Why don't you think it's possible for you?

I was a latch-key kid who never made very good grades, came from a small town and was sent to the military to get my act together. There are normal people like me making millions because we decided to go for it and believed it was possible. I say that to encourage you. Prohibited Profits isn't a difficult concept, it takes bold action.

Instead of worrying about Starbucks, find ways to increase your income. Your salary and savings account won't outgrow the rate of inflation. That $3 cup of coffee will be $6 in a few years. The wealthy don't worry about that. The key is finding ways to make more money.

If you are capped at your current job, think about an opportunity in sales or something on the side that will help you earn extra income. It's far easier to make more money than to save forever, because there will always be unexpected surprises.

A hospital bill, your car breaks down, or your furnace goes out. Even if you save $100 per month on Starbucks, it only takes one accident every five years to wipe out your Starbucks savings. That is not an easy way to sleep at night. If you're buying 10 coffees per day, then maybe there is a different conversation to be had.

Figure out how you can add a high-paying skill to your life. Sell something on commission or document why you deserve a raise at work if that's your only option. It will give you the confidence that you can live and breathe without staring at your bank account. There is something about that confidence that compounds when you start investing.

Maybe you start with $1000 as your initial investment. If you can hit 1000% returns, which happens often, now you have $10,000. If you can duplicate those results, now your $10,000 becomes $100,000. One more time, you hit $1 million. If you compound your results three times, you can turn $1000 into $1 million.

Is that easier said than done, yes. But do you see why I prefer earning more money over cutting out Starbucks? You can invest in more Prohibited Profits opportunities that give you the chance to create financial freedom.

There was once a story I heard, where a spirit asked God, "Father, why didn't you let me win the lottery? I prayed every day for it."

God responded, "Son, you never bought a ticket…"

If you never play the game, then you have 0% chance of winning. If you try, you give yourself an opportunity. I would rather play the game and try to win, than sit on the sidelines to avoid losing. At the end of the day, you lose if you don't play. Get some skin in the game and go for it.

The alternative? Save $100 per month on coffee and hopefully those 10% returns don't encounter an economic crisis anywhere near retirement.

My last disclaimer is this. If you're sitting with no money in your bank account and $30K in credit card debt, do not run to start investing. Your mind will be so scattered because you are already in financial scarcity. You won't make great decisions in scarcity. If a position starts to fall, your brain will go into crazy and you won't be able to stay disciplined.

Focus on increasing your income, get out of debt, or at least get it to a manageable place. Once you do that, then come back to investing. Your financial future will be made by your ability to control your emotions.

CHAPTER 7

PROFITS CHECKLIST

After trading in the markets for more than 20 years, I created a system that would adapt to any Prohibited Profits investment opportunity. The checklist I will share in the book was for crypto. As you will see, the principles will work no matter what the opportunity is in the future.

PRINCIPLE #1: 1000% UPSIDE POTENTIAL

Throughout this book, you have heard me talk about this number 1000%. That is our target for every investment. If I don't believe that an opportunity has the potential to bring back 1000%, it is not investible. In the last year, we have hit 4,600% and have duplicated those results multiple times. These are real numbers and real positions occurring right now.

I like 1000% because it gives us room to pull back our initial investment and still have upside opportunity. For example, once an investment hits 300%, we pull back 1/3 (our initial investment). Now, were playing with profits and risking nothing in the process. We got out of our initial position and now it's easier to sleep at night if the price goes up or down. You are in a zero-risk position.

Once a position hits 1000%, we reassess again. At that point, it's a fantastic problem to have.

Remember, this isn't just crypto related. As we speak, I am growing a tree farm in Central America with these same principles. The initial investment was $10,000 with conservative gains after 10 years being $400,000. Those numbers are conservative at the rate of lumber inflation.

PRINCIPLE #2: PENNY STOCK UPSIDE

Remember the example I shared earlier? About investing in Bitcoin in 2009. If you would have been an early adopter and put $100 into Bitcoin, you would be a billionaire today. That is the power of the compound effect for an investor. If a position goes from $.01 to $.02, you earn the same profits as if it went from $1000 to $2000.

The earlier you can spot an opportunity, the more you have to gain.

When I say penny stock upside, that means it has the opportunity to grow substantially. In the crypto market, this is any investment or coin that is trading under $10. If you can spot an opportunity trading for .12 cents that eventually goes to $12, you stand to make a lot of money. These are opportunities you must hunt for before the mainstream discovers them.

Now, this doesn't mean I am not still buying Bitcoin or the other stablecoins and more expensive assets. But my new opportunities typically fall into the penny stock upside.

PRINCIPLE #3: NO BANKRUPTCY RISK

Bankruptcy risk is very important when looking at a Prohibited Profits opportunity. Typically, where there is high upside, there is also risk. Let me give you a real-world example in the crypto industry.

XRP took a 93% market drop which is nearly unheard of. They were crushed by the SEC and their investors lost most of their money overnight. They basically created 100 billion ripple overnight, which is a huge red flag. They probably should have been sued sooner. That's a great example of a bankruptcy risk.

Ripple is also a great example of opportunity cost and inexperience tax as well. Ripple wasn't always an SEC liability. At one point it was a Prohibited Profits opportunity. In 2017, Ripple was trading at .15 cents and we held it until it reached $3.64 cents. They hadn't yet created money out of thin air and the project had potential.

Then they went through a partnership change, the technology changed, and it wasn't the same coin after that. The bankruptcy risk changed.

So, if you heard Ripple was good because you were listening in 2017, that doesn't mean that it was still good a year later. That is why it's so important to stay up to date on trends, leadership and technology changes.

Enron is another example of the danger associated with investing in bankrupt risk companies.

PRINCIPLE #4: MAGNET FOR FRESH CAPITAL (M0, M1 & M2 MONEY)

This was a huge driving force for Bitcoin. As banks and hedge funds began to adopt Bitcoin on their own balance sheets, the price began to run.

What do I mean M0, M1 & M2? These are places people keep their money. For example, we have money in bank accounts, savings accounts and retirement accounts. Most of the money comes from these M0, M1 & M2 accounts.

The reason why crypto is such a magnet for fresh capital right now is because we are now starting to flow into M1 money. These are institutional dollars ETFs retirement funds and Bitcoin IRAs. It's the institutions way of giving a blessing to Bitcoin and allowing a whole new level of money to flow into it. That is why Bitcoin and crypto have become the sexy new opportunity in the marketplace.

No matter what the opportunity is, look for high upside opportunities that are a magnet for fresh capital. This could be a new investor, a partnership, a shift in legislature or new research. Again, this is why you must act fast, because the news moves fast.

This is why research is so important. I follow companies, big CEO's and watch the conversations that are happening. If you read between context clues, you can find hints at new partnerships or news that may be worth millions to the right investor.

PRINCIPLE #5: IMMEDIATE CATALYST: NEWS, PARTNERSHIPS, BREAKTHROUGHS

Principle 4 and 5 work together often. For example, a few months ago while writing this book the U.S. Government gave their blessings for people to operate in blockchain technology. When the news broke, it wasn't a mainstream headline, but it was valuable to anyone paying close attention. This was a huge catalyst because it opened the blockchain to thousands of banks and became a magnet for fresh capital.

Another good example for future Prohibited Profits is the news cycle surrounding Psilocybin. More research is validating its effectiveness on all kinds of addictions and its mental health benefits. If you are an investor paying attention, it's worth tracking these updates as the opportunity becomes more investible to the masses.

These first 5 checklists are vital to locating a Prohibited Profits opportunity. Almost all of our investments match these first 5 guidelines. 1000% returns, penny stock upside, no bankruptcy risk, magnet for fresh capital and an immediate catalyst almost always means there is money to be made. In the next chapter, I will share the next 6 principles and why the investments I make have a utility to them instead of pure speculation.

PRINCIPLE #6: SUPERIOR TECHNOLOGY

To use a non-crypto example, superior technology would be a company like Tesla. Tesla is focused on creating the next generation of products and putting humans into outer space. It was very clear that Tesla was going to be a strong and investible company.

This is also the reason I invested into an Empress Splendor tree farm. These trees have been engineered to mature into full size, lumber ready trees in 10 years. That is superior technology compared to a tree farm that takes 50 years to harvest. That tree farm will return 2000% + inflation at the end of 10 years.

Think outside the box on these types of investments. There was no shortage of personal computers when Apple came into the market. But their advanced technology made them one of the top investments of our lifetime.

Bitcoin and blockchain technology are advancing quickly. There is infinite opportunity for companies that build superior technology over the next few years.

PRINCIPLE #7: MUST SOLVE A REAL PROBLEM

There has been a lot of talk about "community" type investments and Elon Musk has his own agendas. But I never invest in anything that doesn't solve a real problem. A decade ago, Bitcoin solved the problem by creating a universal currency. Today, we don't need another Bitcoin, we need the next technology that solves a problem.

There are currently more than 10,000 coins and counting that are trying to be Bitcoin. There are a lot of money grabs and scams happening every day. I only invest in coins and investments that solve a real problem.

The empress splendor farm was started after a record wild-fire season in 2020. I knew that lumber was in shortage and that wouldn't change in the near future. Remember, most trees take 30-50 years to mature. There is and will continue to be a lumber shortage here in the U.S. I saw lumber as a Prohibited Profits opportunity because it solves a real problem.

PRINCIPLE #8: FIRST MOVERS' ADVANTAGE

The person who knows the right information first AND takes advantage of it, is always the highest paid. Remember the example about Bitcoin. If you would have invested $100 in 2009, your family would be taken care of for generations. First movers' advantage is the key to taking advantage of Prohibited Profits opportunities.

For example, Ethereum was the first technology to have smart contracts. If you were an early, investor into Ethereum, then you are likely very wealthy right now.

Remember, Tesla was the first company to launch the self-driving car and now every company is trying to copy their model. Tesla already won because of first movers' advantage.

Ford was the first automotive company to start the assembly line and they are still reaping the rewards of being first.

When you go first, you either fall flat on your face or you are praised and reap massive rewards. For the first time ever, you have access to these types of investments. During the dot.com boom, it was only for accredited investors. This is your opportunity to take advantage of this Prohibited Profits window.

PRINCIPLE #9: PROVEN MANAGEMENT TEAM

When I invest into an asset, I first look at the management team. I want to see if they have crypto experience, blockchain experience or at the very least, technology experience. You have probably heard the phrase "bet on the jockey before the horse." That is a true statement because the team will determine the upside of a project.

Don't let this confuse you though. Even if the team is great, the project won't be a success unless the technology is great also.

Before I invest into anything, I look up the management team on LinkedIn and do my research. What kind of projects were they working on before? What is their track record?

PRINCIPLE #10: SOCIAL MEDIA PRESENCE

This one is pretty straight forward. Do they have a social media presence? How engaged are they? Do they have an avid fan base?

I know that technology outperforms community every time, but if a coin has a strong following, then it does improve its chances of success.

Follow them on social media and learn as much as you can before investing.

PRINCIPLE #11: MARKET CAP SUPPLY

The last principle only applies to crypto because if there is an infinite supply, then the coin is not valuable. That's why the supply of Bitcoin is 21 million and there will never be more. That is the difference between inflationary vs deflationary currency.

Meanwhile, the U.S. government is printing trillions of fiat dollars and putting them into circulation. You can't just print trillions of dollars of money and give everyone $600, then expect everything to be the same. There has to be a cap at some level.

This list is not the end all be all and not every investment fits all 11 of these principles. This is a guideline that I start with before I invest. For new investors, don't get caught up in research and freeze mode. Some people will research for the rest of their lives and never pull the trigger.

If you do your research and find an opportunity that you believe in, and it fits 9 of these 11, then don't be afraid to invest. If you wait an extra week or month, some of these opportunities will pass you by.

When you feel confident in something, put $1000 into it or an amount that you can afford to lose. Sure, there is a chance you could lose your investment. That's a real-world concept and it happens in every market. However, there is also a high probability it goes up. You only need to hit 1000% 3 times to take $1000 to $1 million. If you do your research, don't forget to buy a ticket to the game.

CHAPTER 8

INVESTOR INSIGHTS

t's easy for us to become emotional when markets are in chaos. If you have invested before, you know the feeling. When things are great, we assume they will stay like that forever. When our investments turn red, it's easy to panic and sell. Humans are emotional beings. Even the most level-headed investor is guilty of making mistakes when times are tough.

Facts and numbers never lie. Numbers always tell the truth about what happened. There is speculation and then there's truth. When you make an investment, you either made money or lost money. So how do we separate human emotion while we are investing? I always say that the best predictor of future performance is to analyze what we have done in the past.

You have probably seen the disclaimer "past results are no guarantee of future results." While that is true, I do believe that the most successful long-term investors study each investment they make. It's easy to remember our wins and discount our losses. But fear and greed won't change the facts of what actually happened.

I recommend that you start an investment journal to begin tracking each investment. Before I make an investment, I make notes so that I can recall those thoughts when analyzing if it was a winner or loser.

What is the price on the day you invested? The starting point of any investing opportunity.

Why are you buying it? I always make sure to detail why I'm buying into that investment. Be as detailed as possible here. I always document how many of the 11-point checklist criteria the trade hits. I also write down my emotions that day, my optimism or skepticism.

My goal is to remember why the trade could be successful, but also why it may fail. Most investors only want to look at the upside. Be willing to poke holes in your investments and consider why it could fail in the future. This understanding will help you look for red or green flags while you are in the investment.

You can't improve what you don't measure. Of course the numbers will always be there, but don't forget to measure your human emotions and thoughts. Also, if you can recognize your mood and thought process, you become more aware in the future.

Perhaps you will start to recognize that when you have a big win, you become too optimistic and your next investment loses. You might notice that you got in a fight with your spouse and your emotions caused you to make a bad decision because you were in a bad mood.

Your journal can be simple or detailed. Personally, I like to be as detailed as possible because I won't remember how I was feeling 90 days from now. I will remember if it met the 11-point criteria, but my mood and thoughts will have changed. You cannot improve what you don't track. You have heard hundreds of people say that before and all of them have a different track record of success.

Your investment career will be different than anyone else. Unless you are hiring someone like me, who can invest for you, then you will always be responsible for your own growth. Even if you have the right investment picks, your success will depend on your consistent growth as a person. Your levelheaded decision making is your biggest asset in this industry.

Start by journaling and documenting everything you can. You will start to notice your own personal patterns and you can pivot in areas where you are making key mistakes.

LOSS AVERSION & UPSIDE RISK

By looking at the numbers, you can also separate myth from facts. In the investment world, you are paid to be right more than you are wrong. That's a fairly easy concept that most people understand. But that's actually a myth. You are not paid to be right; you are paid when you create profits.

In the stock market, that might require you to be right 60% of the time to hit your yearly 7% gains. But Prohibited Profits opportunities are different. We are not looking for 7% gains. We are targeting 1000%+ upside and speculation. You could be a terrible trader and still hit profits because of the volatility and speculation. Now, you could also lose quicker if you don't understand your exit plans.

You could be right 30% of the time and if those 30% are 1000% upside, you are hitting a 3000 ROI. Whereas, if you lost the other 70%, even if those losses are 500%, you are profitable and far outperforming the stock market or 401K plans.

So even if you are wrong more than you're right, you can be an extremely profitable trader in the right markets. As you start to journal and become a better trader, you can start to flip those percentages and grow much faster. That's another reason I am so passionate about having a trading journal.

Most people don't have the discipline to stick to their plan because most investors only look at investing from an X and Y axis point of view. Very few stop to look at the Z axis. What do I mean by that? Very few people reflect on their emotions and the impact emotions have on our success.

As an investor, you are committing to long term success. There are people making real money in these volatile markets. Those people maintain their emotional certainty during times of chaos. That is the challenge, otherwise you will eventually go back to zero. I have seen too many experienced investors lose millions because they had an emotional attachment to a trade or a company. They think they have the secret insight that nobody else understands.

The most difficult thing to predict is human behavior and at times, the markets themselves. We saw market manipulation firsthand, when a group of fund managers decided to prove their power through AMC. At the time, AMC had no business staying in business, but the power of influence is real. If you were looking from the outside, you may have created a firm conviction that AMC would eventually fail.

It's not what you know that hurts you. It's what you know that just ain't so. I always loved that quote, because it keeps me level-headed as an investor. Even if I see 5000% potential upside, I still use the same 11-point checklist. If that trade hits my 30% stop loss, I will pull out and re-evaluate.

You can still be massively successful hitting 30% winners in this market, especially since we are aiming for 1000% upside. it's how you handle those 70% of losers that will be the difference in your success or failure. Create your system, challenge what you think you know and track your emotions by the minute. The best way to remove emotions from the equation is to track each trade and follow your systems no matter what the circumstance might be.

FIAT FAILURES & INFLATION

Depending on when you are reading this book, the U.S. Dollar is on a path to failure. Inflation is at an all-time high and we saw the government print billions of dollars, backed by nothing. You might be reading this thinking "Seth, you're crazy, the government would never let the dollar fail." That would be extremely naïve and trusting, especially if you look at the historical track record of fiat currency.

There have been 152 fiat currencies that have failed due to hyperinflation. The average lifespan was 24.6 years, the median lifespan was 7 years. Eight of those fiat currencies didn't last a decade and 15 of them didn't make it past 1 year. "Seth, that proves that the dollar won't fail because it has been around a lot longer than that." We may be an economic global leader, with leverage to assume massive debt, but it will not last forever. That shift is already beginning.

You may not be aware of it, but next time you go to the grocery store, take note of the cost of milk, eggs and bread. The grain hasn't changed, and the chickens are still laying the same eggs they were 100 years ago. What has changed? The cost of these items and everything else you buy on a daily basis.

While everything we purchase continues to rise in cost, the value of the dollar continues to decrease. Home prices continue to rise, rent is increasing, and the value of the dollar has never been lower.

Now let's look at how the economy works. Who owns the real estate? The wealthy. Why? Because real estate is a deflationary asset. As long as we are still living on this earth and not in the sky like the Jetsons, real estate prices will continue to rise. So while the government continues to print billions of dollars in fiat, that money circulates right back to the wealthy.

The people that understand how Prohibited Profits works, will always have income circulating back to them via rent checks. They own the assets, goods and services that the lower and middle class pay for. You either decide that you want to play the game or let the game play you. Now that you are aware, you get to decide which game you want to play. You get to decide if you want to take radical responsibility for your finances or wait for the dollar to fail.

Cryptocurrency isn't perfect, but the ones with hard cap supplies are superior. The U.S. Dollar has been in place for 100+ years and it is going to fail. Maybe not tomorrow, maybe not 5 years from now, but eventually it will fail. You will either pay for it, or your kids will pay for it.

Don't let your naivety stand in the way of the facts and start to understand what is really happening. You still have time to take advantage of the opportunities in front of you right now. The government continues to steal from its people by printing more money. That money isn't backed by gold, silver or anything at all.

Naysayers like to joke that cryptocurrency is digital dollars. At least it's backed by a hard cap that is beginning to be accepted by the educated investor. The U.S. Dollar is backed by hopes, prayers and IOU's. If you had one million dollars in your bank account today, your bank would not let you walk down and cash it out right now. They would need days to come up with that cash, because they do not have it.

That's also the reason why interest rates are microscopic. They are leveraging your money to buy them time. The banks know they won't have to pay you anything when you keep your money in a savings account. They are leveraging your money to make themselves wealthy.

You can flip that script at any moment, if you decide to take control of your financial future. You will never get rich by keeping your money in a bank account. Your .02%

interest rate is going to lose against the cost of inflation year over year.

Cryptocurrency and real estate are not the only deflationary options. Think about the products that are rising in cost. If you recently built a house, or inquired about building one, you noticed the cost of lumber skyrocketing. Due to inflation and the recent forest fire outbreaks, lumber costs are also rising.

I noticed that trend a few years ago before it hit the point it is at today. Remember, Prohibited Profits opportunities are everywhere. I wanted to stay ahead of the rising lumber costs, so I invested in an empress splendor tree farm in Central America. In a future chapter, I will share my 9-flag theory, so you understand why I chose central America.

The empress splendor tree matures in 10 years. With the rising lumber costs, I wouldn't be surprised if that investment became a 1000% upside investment once the trees mature. Lumber prices have already increased more than 300% with no end in sight. Look for opportunities to hedge against hyperinflation. Even if you still believe in the U.S. dollar, it's smart to look into hedging against inflation. This is risk management 101.

THE DOT.COM BOOM

If you are old enough to remember the dot.com boom, you probably remember the emerging digital and tech companies that made billions. At the time, I was a teenager, so I wasn't able to fully take advantage of that opportunity. But I watched and noticed the trends. I was obsessed with studying those people who built massive wealth during that time.

The dot.com boom had a profound impact on my life because I also noticed the gatekeepers. The average person couldn't take advantage of these opportunities. Only accredited investors could invest at that time. I was fortunate to know a few of the people that were able to make money in that marketplace. They taught me the importance of first movers advantage and learning to be comfortable being uncomfortable.

Those that created massive wealth, shared stories of people that laughed at them for taking these risks. The internet was a bubble, technology was a fad. We were going back to newspapers and magazines in no time. Let me remind you, the world will never go backwards, and technology isn't going away anytime soon. In fact, it's only moving faster, especially with blockchain technology at the forefront.

The people that were able to ignore the outside voices are now retired. Most of them have enough capital and assets to support their family for generations, as long as they pass down the same principles.

If you have a position in crypto right now, you might be hearing some of those same doubters. "You invested into what?" Even with crypto going mainstream, it's still rejected by most of the population. This is another reason why separating emotions will determine your success.

You have to be willing to stand in the fire and be unmoved by those who don't see what you see. Let them talk now. They will be asking you for money in the future. I remember being called an idiot by multiple people for investing into an electric car company called Tesla. Time is on our side and so is the technology. Let time tell the story and don't let yourself be moved by the limited vision of others.

You might even have to stand through some major fires and be willing to look foolish short term. If you remember, there were a lot of winners in the dot.com boom. There were also plenty of losing companies that were swallowed and failed. However, if you got in on one of the Facebook, Amazon, Alibaba type companies, it made up for the losers. That is the opportunity we are in right now. Remember, it's not always about the investment. It's the timing of the investment.

THE LINK EXAMPLE & FIRST MOVERS ADVANTAGE

If you invested into Tesla now, versus 10 years ago, your portfolio will look dramatically different. First movers advantage is essential in fast moving marketplaces because that's where the opportunity is. If you invest in a coin that is $.10 cents that goes to $1, it would need to go from $1 to $10 to create that same profit. Again, $10 to $100. You don't need each investment to break $100 to make a fortune. If you can spot the opportunity early enough, you make create generational wealth.

In January of 2019, there was a technology called LINK that was trading at .30 cents. It wasn't listed on a normal exchange and my students complained that we had to buy it on a lesser known, third party exchange. We recommended a sizeable position and those that acted, reaped the rewards of first movers advantage.

Depending on when you are reading this, Coinbase supports around 300 coins and rising. That's a small number compared to the 10,000+ coins in circulation. I thought that LINK was going to move fast and would become listed on Coinbase. By following my 11-point checklist, I saw the solid technology and the problem it was solving in the marketplace.

LINK was listed on Coinbase and it blew up to $37. That's a 12,000% ROI and every student made 120X on their investment. Keep in mind, our typical target is 10X. This won't happen on most trades, but even if you had 99 loses before LINK, you could potentially still be in the green because of first movers' advantage.

So get comfortable being uncomfortable. Follow your plan and when you see an opportunity to leverage first movers' advantage, do it. You won't be right every time, but you don't need to. Make sure you have diversified risk management so that when these things do happen. Opportunities like LINK will change the trajectory of your life.

Don't let the short-term opinion of others impact your life's legacy. Also, don't let your ego get in the way. Even if you are wrong in the short term, you can always pivot to find the next Prohibited Profits opportunity.

THE VANGUARD STORY

In January of 1960, Paul Feldstein and Edward Renshaw penned an article talking about how passive investors can outperform professional active asset managers. They touted that passive investors can create better results than active investors.

A man named John B. Armstrong disagreed. John B. Armstrong, who went by the assumed name of John Bogle, decided they were wrong. His bias was standing in the way because he had a lot to lose if they were right. John Armstrong was a manager at the Wellington fund, who at the time in 1960, was the oldest and largest mutual fund in the country.

John wrote a scathing article, insulting Paul and Edward. He called them ignorant and flat out wrong. There is more to the story than that, but I want you to understand the lesson. The article tore these guys apart and it took 14 years for John B. Armstrong to change his opinion.

14 years later, John B. Armstrong founded Vanguard funds. John B. Armstrong is now considered and credited as the father of index funds. Today, he runs a $7 trillion index fund. This guy came out and told these guys they were wrong. He was in a position where he was running active investments for investors. He thought these guys were wrong but decided to do the research anyways. His ego could have stood in the way, but he had the courage to admit he was wrong.

He changed his opinion and today, he is known as the man who created index funds. So why am I bringing this up? Because I have been wrong myself. Every person who invests into the markets has made a mistake or missed a blind spot and lost money. We can learn from our own lessons. We can also learn from historical lessons to improve our understanding, as well as our positions.

Don't let your ego of being right, stand in the way of your next opportunity. Even today, I am looking at the next index fund in the crypto space that might put myself out of business as a hedge fund manager. In the next section, I will share that opportunity so you can decide for yourself.

I am always studying the new emerging opportunities that are developing in crypto. There are John B. Armstrong stories happening every single day because of the upside opportunity in crypto right now.

If you took just a few things from this chapter, remember the importance of removing your emotions and tracking everything. Become a practitioner at studying the facts, both with yourself and the trades that you make. When you can remove human emotions from the equation, you won't feel bad when you make a wrong decision. You also won't overleverage yourself when things are going well.

Stick to your system, track every move and look for the next opportunity where you can move first in the marketplace. Remember, this is Prohibited Profits and you will be wrong often. You might even be wrong more than you are right. However, if you stick to your plan, you only need to hit on the right opportunities to change the financial future for yourself and your family.

CRYPTO WEALTH COACH RECOMMENDA-TIONS

"I get what you are saying, but how do you take advantage of these opportunities?"

Information is great. Understanding what to do with that information is completely different. When I make an investment recommendation, I invest my money into the opportunity as well. My livelihood and my family's future are at stake. I do not make one move that I would consider to be a gamble.

Why?

I do the research and understand the important metrics. Beyond my 11-Step checklist, it's important to dig into the companies. I research the CEO's, every white paper, and connect with people working on the project.

Earlier in this chapter, I shared the Vanguard story. That lesson became a story that I included in my write up entry in Crypto Wealth Coach. After each write up, I share exact instructions on how and where to buy each crypto.

Below is an example of the research and detailed writeup I create before investing into a technology. I only share information that I am using to invest my own money, even if the advice might put me out of business.

DEGEN is the index fund for cryptocurrency that I mentioned previously. As a crypto hedge fund manager, DEGEN is the equivalent of index funds in the crypto marketplace. Although I am confident enough to say I outperform the index funds. DEGEN is a potentially less volatile and highly profitable option. I have already invested in DEGEN myself.

NEW COIN RECOMMENDATION: MINT DEGEN (DEGEN)

Dear VIPs,

In January 1960, Paul Feldstein and Edward Renshaw turned the investing world upside down...

In a four-page white paper, the college student and college lecturer laid out a controversial theory. They showed that passive investors could do just as well as professional asset managers by buying "a company dedicated to the task of following a representative average."

Their work was published in the prestigious Financial Analysts Journal.

Almost immediately, the journal published a scathing rebuttal by John Bogle, a manager at Wellington Fund, one of the oldest and largest mutual funds at the time. Under the pen-name John B. Armstrong, Bogle attempted to refute the article's findings. He refused to believe that passive investments could compete with active management.

If you've heard of Bogle, you know where this story is headed...

Just 14 years later, Bogle founded mutual fund giant Vanguard Funds – which lets investors buy funds that passively mimic indexes.

Today, Bogle is widely credited as being the father of index funds. And these funds hold more than $7 trillion of investors' wealth.

Investors now have the choice of whether they want actively managed or passively managed funds. For many investors, success or failure is now determined by picking the right sectors at the right time.

Now, the investing world is turning upside down again...

One crypto project is creating passive funds that are somewhat actively managed by smart contracts and the investors. I'm talking about decentralized, real-time-weighted index investing... and the community itself votes to include or remove holdings.

With just one investment, we can own a portfolio of 11 crypto projects with big growth potential. We think 1,000% gains are possible.

So let's get started...

Introducing Index Tokens

As cryptocurrency investors, we look at investments differently...

We're investing in an asset class that the mainstream doesn't understand. While everyone else is thinking right versus left, we also look up and down. In other words, we look beyond the "x" and "y" investment plane to see the "z" plane.

That's what we're doing this month...

Instead of just looking at the "x" of passive investing and the "y" of active investing – we're looking at an active passive investment.

You see, it's now possible for a smart contract that anyone can access to hold a specific basket of investments. While this alone would make any passive indexer proud, the smart contract also intelligently and actively manages balances and exposures by rules that would please any active manager.

It's the crypto version of an index fund... and the result turns out to be smarter, easier, and lower cost than buying the same basket of tokens ourselves.

It's all through Indexed. Finance.

Indexed. Finance is a decentralized portfolio management protocol that uses "Index Tokens" to represent the combined value of underlying assets within a pool. In short, the values of multiple tokens are aggregated into one representative token.

Each individual asset within the pool is assigned a targeted weight based on the square root of its market cap. The smart contract then compares this to the asset's current weight and automatically rebalances the pool as people join and leave it. The targeted weight of each asset is also recalculated periodically to maintain an equal and fair distribution within the index pools.

Anyone who owns an Index Token owns a fraction of each of the underlying assets it's tied to. Indexed. Finance has no control over the underlying assets within each Index Token pool. Because of this, owners of Index Tokens are free to "burn" their balance to redeem any of the tokens that make up the pool for each index for a small fee.

For example, if you have an Index Token that represents tokens XXX, YYY, and ZZZ, you could burn your balance to redeem any one of those three tokens or all three in a fair distribution determined by their current value. This is an important feature that may create opportunities for additional profits.

Governance for the Indexed. Finance protocol is ruled by the entire community of users who vote on proposals for updates and changes to the protocol itself over time.

In short, just like with stock and bond index funds, Index Tokens make it easy and cost effective to buy a basket of cryptos. But unlike with traditional index funds, Index Tokens allow for changes to the underlying investments and weightings in the pool based on community votes.

And right now is a great time to buy. You see, thanks to the recent volatility, we're seeing a buyer's market for many cryptos. Virtually, any top project can be bought for $0.30 to $0.50 on the dollar from where they were just 60 to 90 days ago. Patient, contrarian investors know that selective bets made when the market is in pain can pay off handsomely.

That brings us to...

THE DEGEN INDEX (DEGEN) TOKEN

There are currently seven Index Tokens available through Indexed. Finance. But the DEGEN Index (DEGEN) token has us the most excited.

The idea for the DEGEN Index spawned from Twitter, where a user described the need for an index consisting of high-risk, high-reward decentralized finance ("DeFi") crypto projects. These projects would have small market caps and large potential upside.

The idea quickly garnered a significant amount of interest...

As we've written before, DeFi has created "trustless" transactions that will change banking as we know it through peer-to-peer lending, decentralized margin trading, stablecoins, and yields that are impossible for banks to offer.

Over the past 12 months, DeFi projects grew from $1 billion in total value locked in to as high as $86 billion. They currently sit around $60 billion in total value locked in. This is the picture of a "high risk, high reward."

A few weeks after its conception, the DEGEN community decided on Indexed. Finance as the perfect platform to host the token. On January 29, 2021, a proposal was submitted to the Indexed. Finance community for DEGEN's creation.

Originally, the proposal listed 30 different tokens, but it was whittled down by the community over time. After the proposal was approved in February and brought to market in March, only 11 tokens remained.

Side Note: "Degen" is commonly used as a truncated version of the word "degenerate." But it doesn't mean there's anything degenerate about this investment.

Like many words, degen has morphed in meaning. It's like how the word "criminal" can describe someone involved in an illegal activity, or as an exaggeration of how good something is.

So degen may have connotations of "degenerate gambler" or someone who'd do anything to make a fast buck... but it has been co-opted by crypto investors who are trying to capture the feeling of outrageous possible returns. An important distinction!

Indexed. Finance describes DEGEN as a high-risk, high-reward Index Token comprised of Ethereum protocols that demonstrate the potential for substantial growth over time. In short, DEGEN is a laser-focused portfolio of DeFi projects hyper-tuned for growth.

The 11 DeFi-based tokens are:

    I. Reserve Rights (RSR)
    II. 1inch (1INCH)
    III. RenVM (REN)
    IV. Curve DAO (CRV)
    V. BadgerDAO (BADGER)
    VI. Alpha Finance Lab (ALPHA)
    VII. Polkastarter (POLS)
    VIII. Ocean Protocol (OCEAN)
    IX. Wrapped MIR (WMIR)
    X. Rari Governance Token (RGT)
    XI. THORChain (RUNE)

According to Indexed. Finance, these projects all met the criteria below:

A. The token has a market cap ranging from $50 million to $2 billion (calculated by a rolling 14-day time-weighted average price on Uniswap).
B. This token is at least a week old.
C. No major vulnerabilities have been discovered in the token contract.
D. The token's supply cannot be arbitrarily inflated or deflated maliciously.
E. The control model should be considered if the supply can be modified through governance decisions. The token also does not have transfer fees or other non-standard balance.
F. Updates.
G. The token meets the requirements of the ERC-20 standard.
H. Sufficient liquidity is locked in the Uniswap market pair between the token and wrapped ETH (WETH). (This does not apply to WETH.)

I. The token is one of:

+ Protocol token for an Ethereum-based project.
+ Governance token for a DeFi project.
+ Wrapper token for a blockchain's native currency.

These criteria ensure that the pool will function. But the reason DEGEN token holders expect high returns is because of the potential upside for each token.

So let's take a look at the underlying assets of the DEGEN Index token...

1INCH (1INCH)

Long-standing VIP members should be familiar with 1inch... it's a decentralized exchange ("DEX") aggregator. When someone wants to make an exchange on a DEX between two tokens, 1inch helps find the best price with the lowest fees.

You see, exchange rates on DEXs aren't fixed, so the more you exchange, the worse the exchange rate can get. The market can also easily be moved in tokens with low liquidity. This is called "price slippage."

1inch automatically assesses the current rates and liquidity on DEXs and finds you the best exchange rate. In short, 1inch aims to make the entire DEX process more user-friendly.

1INCH is the governance token for the 1inch protocol. Holders of 1INCH can vote on proposals for rewards, swapping fees, price impact fees, and more.

There are currently more than 60,000 1INCH token holders on the Ethereum blockchain. And the 1inch team is distributing tokens through airdrops over a period of four years. Users who meet certain requirements like completing four swaps for a total of $20 are eligible for the airdrops.

1inch is currently the 10th largest DEX and trades more than $150 million per day. But we think it will only grow from here.

RESERVE RIGHTS (RSR)

Reserve Rights is building a decentralized stablecoin to create a global safe place for people to store (or "reserve") their money.

As most of us know too well, central banks in many countries can't always be trusted. Some governments run up insane deficits and print large sums of new currency, destroying their citizens' purchasing power in the process. Reserve Rights is attempting to solve this problem.

But that's not the only problem Reserve Rights is trying to fix... The team believes that anyone in the world should be able to transact with anyone else without an intermediary.

The Reserve Protocol uses three different types of tokens. The Reserve token (RSV) is a stablecoin pegged to the

U.S. dollar to maintain a fixed value. RSV is meant to be a decentralized currency that can't be manipulated or abused by a government or central bank.

RSV's peg is maintained through an automated stability protocol that uses a second type of asset-backed token as collateral to cover the total value of RSV tokens. If the price of RSV drops below $1, the protocol purchases more RSV for tokenized assets to bring the value back up. Likewise, if it rises above $1, the protocol sells newly minted RSV for tokenized assets.

The third type of token used by the protocol is the Reserve Rights token (RSR). Its main purpose is to facilitate the stability of the RSV stablecoin by guaranteeing its collateralization rate and peg to the U.S. dollar. In short, the Reserve Protocol mints and sells new RSR tokens for additional collateral tokens to make sure the RSV token's total value remains fully covered. But RSR is also used as the governance token for the Reserve protocol, allowing its holders to launch and vote on proposals.

There are around 50,000 RSR token holders on the Ethereum blockchain. And that number should increase as the Reserve Protocol grows.

RenVM (REN)

Originally called "Republic Protocol," the RenVM network allows users to transfer value between networks by providing inter-blockchain liquidity. Users can interact with multiple assets and chains in one transaction. Essentially, the network brings cross-chain interoperability to the world of decentralized finance ("DeFi"). The REN token is required as a bond to register and run a node on the RenVM network. There are currently more than 52,000 REN holders on the Ethereum blockchain.

For example, if someone wanted to use their bitcoin on the Ethereum network, they would "lock" their bitcoin into RenVM. Then Ren would send a "minting signature" for the original depositor to sign, which usually happens automatically through the protocol. After that, the depositor receives renBTC to their Ethereum wallet of choice, which can be traded or used in DeFi protocols as an ERC-20 token on the Ethereum network. Since launching last summer, RenVM has grown significantly. It recently passed $4.5 billion in cross-chain volume on its network. The growth is accelerating too... It took 144 days for RenVM to pass $1 billion... 87 days after that to hit $2 billion... 44 days after that to hit $3 billion... and just 37 days to go from $3 billion to $4 billion in total chain volume.

CURVE DAO (CRV)

Curve is a decentralized autonomous organization ("DAO") focused on providing liquidity between stablecoins on the Ethereum network. It aims to solve price slippage and liquidity issues that occur using other automated stablecoin exchanges.

With Curve, users and smart contracts can exchange stablecoins like Dai (DAI) and USD Coin (USDC). Curve also lets liquidity providers ("LP") form pools to earn fees.

Curve is the go-to automated market marker ("AMM") when it comes to trading between stablecoins because it has the lowest slippage between like assets and also boasts the lowest trading fees. Liquidity providers for Curve's pools receive the trading fees, as well as rewards paid out in the CRV token.

The CRV token is used by Curve for governance. Holders of CRV can vote on proposals, and the longer they hold their CRV tokens, the more voting power they have. LPs for the Curve protocol are paid in CRV at a rate that decreases annually.

In early June, Curve released a whitepaper for its V2. Previously, Curve only facilitated trading between like assets (i.e., coins that in theory have the same intrinsic value). But with its newest proposal, Curve will open a three-crypto pool between WETH, Wrapped Bitcoin (WBTC), and Tether (USDT). This pool is a bullish indicator for Curve since it will now compete directly with Uniswap.

In February, Curve announced that it passed $4 billion in deposits. This made it one of the largest DEXs in the world. Since then, Curve has added more than $2 billion in deposits, bringing its total value locked to nearly $8 billion. There are more than 35,000 CRV holders on the Ethereum blockchain alone. And Curve's recent integrations with the Fantom and Polygon blockchains signal that it still has a lot of room for growth.

OCEAN PROTOCOL (OCEAN)

The Ocean Protocol wants to "unlock the value of data." Through its Ocean Market, users can securely and privately buy, sell, and trade data assets. Essentially, Ocean has built a decentralized exchange for data instead of cryptocurrencies. It accomplishes this through ERC-20 "datatokens," which are minted and deployed to represent various types of data assets. Users can consume these datatokens by spending them through the protocol.

When a provider wants to create its own datatoken, it must specify different fields to mint and publish the token on Ocean's marketplace. This includes a title, description, price, and a URL that specifies where the data can be found. When a buyer is interested in a datatoken, they can purchase and redeem the token to receive a downloadable link that leads to the dataset requested – as long as they're connected through the same wallet used to make the purchase. Some of the Ocean Market's most-traded assets are things like consumer browsing data and listings on sites like Amazon and eBay.

Ocean's native token, OCEAN, is the default token used for buying and selling datatokens in the Ocean Market. People can also use OCEAN to stake various data assets and vote on proposals as a governance token. The token's price is based on its usage rate.

There are currently more than 30,000 OCEAN token holders. But as more people interact with the marketplace, this number should rise.

BADGERDAO (BADGER)

BadgerDAO is focused on bringing bitcoin to DeFi through its bitcoin-pegged token DIGG. DIGG auto-rebases to keep it loosely tied to the price of bitcoin. BadgerDAO also integrated RenVM to offer a bitcoin bridge from bitcoin to renBTC or WBTC.

Once you've bridged the gap from the Bitcoin blockchain, BadgerDAO enables its users to deposit their bitcoin-pegged assets to earn on them through Sett Vaults, which are tokenized bitcoin vaults that utilize automated strategies across multiple DeFi platforms to produce yield.

The protocol offers impressive annual returns on investment ("ROI") for depositing the DIGG token into a vault, as well as multiple rewards through other deposits.

For example, depositing a SushiSwap-Wrapped BTC-interest-bearing BTC liquidity pair (SLP-IBBTC-WBTC) into a vault on the BadgerDAO protocol rewards the depositor with SUSHI, BADGER, DIGG, and SushiSwap LP fees. Altogether, the ROI adds up to a substantial 28% to 63% annual return.

BadgerDAO has been "community owned from day one." And it plans to stay that way through publicly released auditing reports of its smart contracts, as well as governance voting through its native token BADGER.

As long as bitcoin remains the top cryptocurrency in terms of market cap, protocols like BadgerDAO will be necessary to bridge the gap between bitcoin and DeFi. And with more than 25,000 BADGER token holders, it's clear that BadgerDAO is accumulating a significant community of users.

ALPHA FINANCE LAB (ALPHA)

Alpha Finance Lab is a system of DeFi products that work together to provide competitive yield rates, minimized risk, and convenience for liquidity providers and yield farmers.

It has three main platforms for yield farming and LPs. Two of these are built on the Ethereum blockchain, Alpha Homora and Alpha Homora V2. The third, also called Alpha Homora, is built on the Binance Smart Chain.

Currently, there is around $1 billion total value locked across all three platforms.

By providing liquidity pairs to the Alpha Homora products (like UNI-ETH or BNB-CAKE), LPs can earn substantial yields from 30% to 300%. These liquidity pairs are leveraged to increase trading-fee annual percentage rates ("APRs"). It's also possible to participate in leveraged yield farming through token pairs, which pay out additional native tokens for DeFi protocols like Curve DAO (CRV) or SushiSwap (SUSHI). These tokens are automatically reinvested through the Alpha Homora protocol to increase yield farming and trading fee APRs. LPs and yield farming through the Alpha Homora platforms also accrue Alpha's native token, ALPHA.

ALPHA powers the Alpha Tokenomics product. Through Alpha Tokenomics, users can stake their ALPHA to receive rewards and unlock higher leverage on the Alpha Homora products. The highest rank, Alpha Pack Leader, can be obtained by staking 1 million or more ALPHA. This unlocks 40% higher leverage on the Alpha Homora V2 platform.

There are currently around 6,000 ALPHA holders on Ethereum, so it still has a lot of room for growth as the Alpha Finance team continues to build out their products.

POLKASTARTER (POLS)

Polkastarter is a decentralized cross-chain protocol that lets new projects raise capital and build a community through token pools and auctions. Polkastarter is built on Polkadot, a platform focused on security, scalability, and interoperability.

What really sets Polkastarter apart is the due diligence and research the team puts into each project listed on the platform.

You see, countless DeFi projects are launched without much thought or planning behind them. This can lead to dead projects very quickly.

Polkastarter also offers fixed ratio swaps, which limit the amount an individual investor can invest and encourages a fair distribution of tokens.

POLS is the native governance token of Polkastarter. It's responsible for whitelisting investors and enabling them to purchase tokens for an initial decentralized offering. The token is available on both Ethereum and Binance Smart Chain.

This process is regulated through a ticketing system, where every 250 POLS equal one ticket that is whitelisted at random. The more tickets you have, the higher chance you have of participating. Another way to get tickets is through providing liquidity to either the Uniswap ETH-POLS or

PancakeSwap BNB-POLS pools. LP tokens count as 100 POLS each. So five LP tokens equal 500 POLS, or two tickets.

There are around 40,000 POLS token holders on the Ethereum blockchain alone, with around 3,500 holders on the Binance Smart Chain. And since late 2020, Polkastarter has already successfully launched more than 100 projects through its token pool system, with many more on the way.

WRAPPED MIR (WMIR)

Wrapped MIR is a Mirror Protocol (MIR) token that has been "wrapped" in an Ethereum smart contract.

You see, the MIR token is native to the Terra (LUNA) ecosystem. By wrapping the token, it can trade on the Ethereum blockchain and exchanges like 1inch and Uniswap.

Mirror Protocol tracks the price of stocks, futures, exchange-traded funds, and other traditional financial assets. Then it lets users mint synthetic assets – known as Mirrored Assets ("mAssets") – that "mirror" the price behavior of the real-world assets by reflecting the exchange prices on-chain. Mirror Protocol is the first protocol to do this.

Mirror's goal is to provide investment options to people who have been disenfranchised from global financial systems. Using Mirror, anyone in the world can invest in synthetic assets tracking top U.S. stocks.

New assets, beyond the initial 12 synthetics tracking the most popular U.S. technology stocks, can be introduced by anyone holding MIR tokens – the governance token of the Mirror Protocol. The proposal is then put to a vote, and if the DAO passes the proposal, the new asset is added.

We believe Mirror's goal of creating synthetic assets for global buyers could become one of the biggest opportunities in crypto.

There are currently around 24,000 holders of WMIR on the Ethereum blockchain. Owning the token controls whether you can use Mirror, so the token value will rise as the world discovers their power.

RARI GOVERNANCE TOKEN (RGT)

RGT is the governance token for DAO Rari Capital.

Rari Capital is an online service designed to make DeFi easier for people who want to build their own wealth. It lets individuals easily earn safe yields on stable investments with less risk.

After Rari launched, it expanded to offer leveraged yield-farming strategies, and now it lets investors of any risk level access yield-earning solutions.

Rari optimizes yields from a variety of asset pools, including stable assets and lending or farming, across various DeFi protocols like Compound and Aave. RGT is used to vote on proposals made by other token-holding community members or to create proposals. Token holders will eventually be able to delegate their voting power to another address to pool voting power. Every aspect of Rari Capital is controlled by the governance mechanism, which also controls token buybacks and burns that can increase the token value by lowering supply.

RGT is notable thanks to its so-called "fair launch," where the DAO chose not to sell any tokens as part of its initial launch. Instead, it gave tokens out to liquidity miners who supported the protocol and the founding team.

Rari's future plans include cross-chain bridges, which could help Rari achieve its end-goal of attracting all of DeFi's liquidity (currently $58 billion). This is a big goal, but we believe Rari could grow quickly. There are currently around 10,000 RGT holders on the Ethereum blockchain.

THORCHAIN (RUNE)

THORChain is a decentralized platform that allows anyone in the world to trade one digital asset on one chain with another digital asset on another chain. Put simply, it's like Uniswap, but multi-chain.

However, RUNE is being phased out of DEGEN. The community determined that its current market cap is too large to warrant inclusion in DEGEN's "high risk, high reward" portfolio.

DEGEN Can Trade at a Premium or Discount

As we've shown, DEGEN isn't merely a representation of an index – some mathematical formula that attempts to track a number. By owning DEGEN tokens, you own the underlying assets. But it's possible for DEGEN to trade at a premium or discount on exchanges.

You see, the price of DEGEN tokens on the exchange doesn't have to be the same as the value of DEGEN. So DEGEN minters who see DEGEN trading on exchanges above the value of the assets could simply sell their DEGEN for a profit and mint themselves more DEGEN tokens to lock in the profit.

You can also burn DEGEN tokens to claim one, several, or even all of these underlying assets. The index fund works in both directions, which investors may be able to use to their advantage if the discount or premium makes sense after paying the Ethereum, exchange, and smart contract fees.

Here's an example of how this works...

If DEGEN is trading for a discount to its NAV on Uniswap, you could buy DEGEN from Uniswap and burn the token to retrieve one of these underlying assets, which could be swapped with ETH for a great value.

If Uniswap lists DEGEN for higher than its NAV, you could mint new DEGEN tokens from one of the 11 underlying assets and sell your new DEGEN to Uniswap for a higher price.

If this strategy sounds a lot like watching the NAV of an exchange-traded fund, you're right. The difference is that with decentralized smart-contract-based funds like DEGEN, you can exchange your tokens for DEGEN and your DEGEN for tokens at any time.

DEGEN RISKS

One benefit of using Indexed. Finance is its commitment to security. Funds locked in an Index Token are unavailable for developers on the team to interact with. The only way to have a claim on the underlying assets of the Index Token is to have the token itself, which can be burned through its smart contract code regardless of whether the user interface is up and running.

However, one risk is if a token is locked in the pool it may not be eligible to receive a staking reward or airdrop... That could mean DEGEN token holders receive less value for their money.

Another risk is simply that one or more of the projects fails to achieve its goals. This risk is possible with any crypto but could be inherently higher with the small- to medium-sized projects DEGEN selects.

Something could also go wrong with one of the underlying assets, like a pump and dump scheme. But Indexed. Finance attempts to safeguard against this risk with a circuit breaker technology that monitors each asset's supply and value. If something gets too unbalanced, it will "pump the brakes" to assure that the value for the Index Token remains relatively stable.

There's also a rebalancing risk. Because DEGEN attempts to maintain a weighted ratio between the component tokens, numerous people could all attempt to mint with the same token at the same time – forcing the pool to sell that token repeatedly. This could cause a temporary dip in the token you're minting and increase the fees that you pay.

The final risk to consider is paying a market premium for DEGEN tokens if you buy them on an exchange instead of minting them. Buying the tokens could be much more convenient but overpaying for them could create a temporarily inflated price.

How High DEGEN Could Go?

We're targeting a 10x or 1,000%+ return on DEGEN tokens in 12 to 24 months.

As more and more people learn about DeFi and the technology improves, potentially hundreds of billions of dollars will flow into it. The potential yields are simply too strong. Crypto, and DeFi in particular, used to be a career risk if an institution held it... soon, it will be a career risk not to.

Right now, DeFi projects represent 4.9% of the cryptocurrency market. Meanwhile, financials make up nearly 10% of the market cap of the S&P 500. While you can't strictly compare cryptos to equities, it's clear that DeFi should continue to grow.

And each of the projects in DEGEN are just getting started.

The average market cap of the individual components of DEGEN is less than $350 million. However, the average market cap of the top 20 DeFi tokens right now is over 10 times that amount. That doesn't guarantee us upside, but it shows how high these tokens can go when they catch the market's attention. We believe each of these cryptos could eventually be top-20 projects.

As mentioned above, DEGEN places a weighting target on each index component based on the square root of the market cap.

While that may sound like an unnecessary complication, it's a brilliant touch when you're dealing with extremely volatile investments. Due to the nature of square roots, the larger a crypto's market cap gets, the smaller its influence in the portfolio gets.

Imagine two cryptos... ABCD has a market cap of $4, and EFGH has a market cap of $100.

The square root of $4 is $2, and the square root of $100 is $10. Even though EFGH is 25 times larger than ABCD in real life, its target weighting is only five times larger in the "square root" portfolio.

So smaller market caps can affect the portfolio more. And as a token rockets up in value, the intelligent passive index will reduce the effective size in the portfolio. Meanwhile, if a token drops in value, its weighting should increase proportionally relative to the larger tokens. Essentially, the index takes profits on winners... and buys the dip on underperformers automatically. That's why we want to own DEGEN tokens.

CALL TO ACTION

After sharing all of the research behind each investment, I then share a detailed call to action so that our members know where to invest, how to invest and what to do next. All of these steps are consistent with every investment I make because I am investing my money right alongside my students. As always, I sign off every post with the most important piece of advice I can share with you.

Stay ahead of the masses,

Seth Maniscalco

Founder, Crypto Wealth Coach

YOUR OPPORTUNITY NOW

Why would I share that lengthy write-up with you?

If you are considering investing, get clear on what it takes to be a successful long-term investor. Many people are getting into cryptocurrency because it's the hottest trend. Most of those people will lose all of their money. Not because of the market, but because they weren't prepared for what they were getting into. They either got emotional, short-sighted or didn't have a solid plan.

Investing is not an overnight, get rich quick opportunity. Your goal should be to create long term wealth for generations. If you are investing your hard-earned money, I recommend you put that much research into each investment or hire someone that does. That person doesn't have to be me. Make sure it's someone you trust, that has a track record of success. They should be investing into their own picks and doing detailed research on the companies they recommend

Once you start earning 1000%+ returns, become financially literate on how you can keep more money. Cryptocurrency isn't tax free and you still have to pay your capital gains taxes if you withdrawal money. Make sure to consult with an accountant to see what opportunities are available to you.

In the next chapter, I will share the 9-flag theory on how to keep more of the profits you make. Remember, it's not how much money you make. It's how much money you get to keep.

CHAPTER 9

9-FLAG THEORY

I t's not about how much money you make, it's about how much money you can keep and how much money you can compound. Tax laws here in the U.S. are complicated for a reason. If the U.S. government can keep you confused and afraid, then they own you. Ignorance is not bliss. Ignorance is financial suicide and the only person to blame is yourself.

There are millionaires and billionaires that pay next to nothing in taxes because they understand how tax laws work. There are ways that you can save more money if you are educated or hire a CPA that is already educated.

Saving and compounding money isn't just about understanding tax laws. There are other ways to reduce your risk of governments, their dollars and regulations that might stop you in your tracks.

Originally, this theory was called the 3-flag theory, then there was a 5-flag theory. I have spent my entire life studying ways to keep more of my money. Before I share these 9 flags, I want to make something clear.

I am a proud American, a marine and I gladly and willingly pay the taxes I owe. But I'm not ignorant about how poorly the government is running the financial future of this country. No matter your political affiliation, this is about your finances and family's livelihood.

If your only residency is in the U.S. and your only currency is the U.S. Dollar, then you are at the mercy of the government's decisions. Now, I don't think the U.S. government is going to do a bail in. I don't think they will become insolvent overnight. But I do believe you should protect yourself and diversify that risk.

Bitcoin begins to solve that problem because it's a different currency. If you have a tree farm in Nicaragua, now you're dealing with their currency. By having real estate outside of the U.S. that property is not taxable. You could go purchase a $400,000 home in Panama and the U.S. government cannot tax you. Most people don't know or understand that.

FLAG #1: Have a second residency

FLAG #2: Have a second citizenship in another country, separate from your second residency

For the reasons I just shared, it's important to have a second residency and a second citizenship in a different country. You have different laws and different opportunities if you have a second residency in one country and a second citizenship in another.

Outside of the tax benefits, there are certain restrictions that don't apply to you if you have a second citizenship in another country. Make sure your second citizenship is in a different country than your second residency. You might want to get a second residency somewhere like Panama and citizenship in Nicaragua.

FLAG #3: Where is your business located?

If you are selling t-shirts or products online, then you may need to have your business based in the U.S. However, if you are running an online business, which is ideal, then having an offshore business is completely legal and comes with a different tax jurisdiction. These laws are always changing and moving, so please stay up to date.

There are many countries that give you the freedom to operate your business differently.

FLAG #4: Where are your banks?

If you are thinking about diversifying correctly, then you should consider having your bank in a different country than your residency. For example, if your bank was in Cyprus during the bail in, you would have lost a lot of money because your bank was located in that country. A savvy investor would have seen that the Cyprus government was on a path to insolvency.

If you think the U.S. dollar may one day crash and the government might be in trouble, then consider having your bank in a different country from your residency.

FLAG #5: Where are you hosting your website?

There are more than 200 countries where you can host your website. The U.S. government claims to be a free country, but freedom of speech isn't always backed by the U.S. government. Especially when talking about Bitcoin and controversial topics. There is a risk that your website could disappear overnight.

For me, I host my website in Iceland because their freedom of speech laws are a lot more flexible. Remember, I'm talking about controversial businesses, not illegal ones. If you are running an online Ponzi-scheme, it's not going to help you to host your business in Iceland. But if you are in a controversial business, consider your options.

FLAG #6: Where do you vacation?

If you have a residency in Panama and a residency in Nicaragua, then vacation elsewhere in a different country. When you're on vacation in Sweden, you're going to get treated differently because you are a visitor in another country.

FLAG #7: Where do you store your gold?

Gold is an asset and a great one to hold. It's also very expensive to store and if you keep it in the U.S. you run the risk of it being repossessed in the United States. You've got to look at how secure the banking industries are in certain countries. I don't recommend storing gold here in the U.S.

For me, I recommend a place like Singapore because it will be a lot cheaper and it's not at risk of being repossessed.

It might sound silly, but in the 1930's the U.S. government outlawed gold and everyone had to turn their gold in. If you had your gold stored in a different country, this didn't apply to you. This also applies to any precious metals you might hold.

FLAG #8: Where is your real estate?

International real estate is tax free unless it's an asset. Look into your countries tax laws and consult your CPA because real estate tax laws are constantly changing. As of now, you can purchase real estate in a different country and the U.S. government cannot tax you.

FLAG #9: Where are your trademarks?

If you are someone that deals in trademarks, I recommend somewhere like Luxembourg because of their secure and supportive trademark laws.

We could go a lot deeper into each of these flags, but this book is not about each of the flags individually. This book is about understanding that there are alternatives to what you currently know about banking, taxes and laws. All of these flags are completely legal. There is nothing the government can do if you decide to exercise your rights.

Most importantly, I wanted to share these flags, so you begin to question every belief about money and finances. Times are changing, the world is moving more online and laws are constantly being updated.

Remember, Prohibited Profits is about educating yourself. Commit to being responsible for every part of your future.. If your business is on Facebook only, and your Facebook page is banned, then you are out of business. Make sure that you understand your rights and how to protect your money, while saving more of it.

Some of these flags might sound like a lot of work. But if you are making millions of dollars, these small changes will save you millions over your lifetime. For me, that is everything because ever dollar I save, can be compounded into the next Prohibited Profits opportunity. Every dollar counts when it can be put back into another 1000% up-side opportunity.

CHAPTER 10

KEEPING PROFITS

If you're new to investing, then numbers like 1000% up-side probably excite you. You might also be asking, what about the downside potential? Is it easier to lose all of your money as well?

Prohibited Profits opportunities do carry more risk than a 401K or traditional stock might. It's easy to be an investor when things are going well. The best investors in the world are able to control their emotions when things get challenging.

During the writing of this book, there was one day where Bitcoin dropped from 60K to $36K. For most investors, and especially new investors, that is a doomsday scenario. Your mind starts to race, and it can be difficult to see where the run stops. I've been there, trust me.

"Be greedy when others are fearful and fearful when others are greedy."

I always loved that quote because 99% of people invest with their emotions. As soon as the numbers turn red, they want to get out before they lose everything. On the other hand, some optimistic investors never think a run is coming to an end. They think the party will go on forever.

Emotions are the enemy for a long-term successful investor.

That's why it's essential that you have an exit plan before you ever invest. If you remember our strategy, I recommend pulling back my original investment after a trade has hit 300% returns.

My mind knows that we are riding with profits now and have a zero-risk exposure, while our investment could go up another 700% or more. If it goes to zero, I didn't lose a dime because I bought out of my original position.

As for my losses, it depends on whether I still believe in the asset. Has something has changed that caused the decline? Let's say a company had bad press, but I still believe in their technology. I might invest more because I believe that the news will eventually turn positive again. There are also situations like Ripple. When things change dramatically, you should re-examine the opportunity.

Your exit plan is your contingency that will answer all of the "what ifs" once you make your investment. Set up these guidelines before you invest and stick to them no matter how difficult it might be in the moment. If you are holding an asset and it starts to spike, you might want to sell and lock in profits and vice versa.

Your buy and sell exit plans should be based on your risk tolerance. For some people, they want to invest in riskier, upside potential. These investors are looking for that 1 or 2 big wins to offset their losses. Other investors may want a more conservative approach.

The biggest challenge for investors is the concept of FOMO (Fear Of Missing Out). Let's say you are holding a coin and it has jumped 1200%. Your exit-plan says to sell after it hit 1000% but everyone in the news and your friends, say they won't sell. They it's going to continue to rise and they are already planning to buy that yacht.

These are the moments that define successful and unsuccessful investors. You will hear crypto investors always talking about holding their crypto. That might be a long-term strategy, but your gains are never profits until you sell them. You could be up 3000%, but until you sell, those numbers don't matter. Knowing when to sell and when to hold can be difficult to predict.

Instead of trying to predict the future, set up systems and guidelines before you invest. Also, don't get caught competing with your friends and peers in this game. Remember, your ego won't pay the bills and your friends won't either.

This is a business and unless you run a hedge fund like me, then it's everyone for themselves. Make level headed decisions that will keep you in the game, even if your optimistic mind wants you to hold on forever. The most important part is that you don't waiver from your rules.

If you don't want to spend all day trading from your computer, then set up limit/stop orders that will make sure you stick to your plan. For example, if you buy a crypto at $5, you can set a sell limit to sell once it hits $15. On the other side, you could set a sell limit at $3 to make sure you don't lose your entire investment.

That is how I set up most of my investments, because I started this to spend more time with my family, not less. There are some investors that will drive themselves and their family crazy because of their obsession with watching the numbers. I want you to be financially free, not financially handcuffed to your computer. If you have more questions about setting limits, please reach out or do your own research so you can enjoy your life while making money.

Remember, selling at a high point is a good thing, even if you didn't capitalize on the maximum return. Once you sell, you can move on to the next Prohibited Profits opportunity and reinvest your money. The goal is compound interest and compound growth over time. It's easy to get greedy and lose track of the progress you have made. Be patient, this game of investing is a lifelong challenge. It's a marathon, not a sprint.

Once you lock in profits, that doesn't mean you can't invest into that asset again in the future. If I think one of my investments has maxed out because it is on a hot streak at 1500%, there will probably be some regression. Many people will sell high.

If I sell and lock in 1500% profits, and then it drops over the next few days, I can reinvest at a new position. This is a phrase commonly referred as buying the dip. As soon as I sell, I go back to my 11-point checklist and decide whether I still believe it is a viable project.

Make sure you have a plan, otherwise you won't have the discipline to make calm rational decisions when markets get crazy.

Saving more of your money

The current capital gains taxes will make anyone feel a little bit sick to their stomach. Every day, it feels like the U.S. government is making it more difficult to get wealthy. Yet, there are some people who are still bragging about paying more taxes than they should be. I've mentioned before, that I am proud to be a tax paying American. But I also believe you should use every tax break the government allows.

For example, there is a capital gains tax law. You should consult your CPA, but this law allows you to write off over 33% of your capital gains if you invest them into an asset.

There are laws in place to help you keep your wealth, instead of giving it to the government. This is available because you educated yourself on the laws. Somebody is paying $100,000 in taxes that they could have saved, by making a down payment on a $300,000 home instead.

Now, instead of losing that money, you can invest it into another asset that will help you compound your wealth. Maybe you rent that house out, so now they are paying your mortgage and you have an appreciating asset.

This is why I'm also a big believer in real estate. The U.S. government declares real estate an asset and there are huge tax advantages to buying real estate. These are Prohibited Profits mindsets that you will want to adopt.

Pay your share of the taxes, but make sure you are not overpaying or being ignorant with your money. Remember, we are committing to taking full responsibility for our financial freedom. Not knowing these laws will cost you millions over your lifetime.

Remember, those who understand compound interest, earn it. While those who don't, pay it.

CHAPTER 11

PROHIBITED DECISIONS

I watched my 2 oldest kids grow up from the road. I remember the pain I felt living out of hotels and saying goodnight over the phone every night. I felt like I was letting them down as a father because I couldn't be there for them. It was easier to justify because I was working for them, but I knew that I had to break the family cycle.

Remember, my parents never around because they were always busy working. My parents made just enough to get by and just enough to buy that little house of their dreams. I wasn't supposed to create generational wealth. The system was not set up for a guy like me to succeed, much less run a hedge fund.

I am a mid-western man with a military background and some tattoos that match the stories, along with the values of my life. I come from a long list of hard workers that worked their entire life just to get by. I've seen what hard work looks like and what working hard looks like. 99% of the people like me, never decide to change their life. They keep going to that job, every single day until they retire or get fired.

There was a real possibility that I could have ended up fulfilling that story. I was well on track with my 401K and benefits plan. But every day I spent away from my kids made me more determined than ever to find a way. I had to get pissed off at my situation and do whatever it took to change my life.

I think everyone should have that main character moment. That moment in the movie where Rocky gets knocked down for the last time and decides to get pissed off. The moment he decides to wipe off the blood and start punching back. It's time to get mad and get moving. I hope that my story inspires you but also makes you angry.

I am not a Harvard grad and I wasn't handed money to start my career. But I did decide to change my story and my life. I made the decision to do something bold. If I didn't believe in the 401K system, then I was going all in on Bitcoin. No matter what happened after that I was committed to a new path.

Before the end of this book, I want to ask you about the story you are currently living in. There are likely people you see living the life of your dreams. Take some time to reflect on the story that is keeping you from going for it. For me, it was my wife and kids. I said, "what if I fail and I can't support my family?"

The only way I would let my family down, is if I didn't go all in on our future. I wasn't being a great father or husband because I was gone all of the time. I made the decision to be fully committed and to bet on myself. That started with learning to trust myself.

Most people never bet on themselves because they can't fully trust themselves. If you lost your job tomorrow, do you believe you would starve? Or would you find a way?

Most people choose security because it's safe. Very few people want the pressure of providing for their family alone. I'm not asking you to quit your job overnight. But I am saying that you could, and you would find a way if you are hungry for change. I had to learn how to trust myself, because I was about to invest my entire 401K into Bitcoin.

There is a reason they don't teach financial literacy in schools. They don't want you to understand how the system of wealth works. If everyone knew these secrets, the banks would go bankrupt. They key is starting to educate yourself on how money and finances work. If everyone has a 401K, then it's only worth what the government says it's worth, as we have seen during multiple crashes.

If you are betting on the U.S. government over yourself, then this book has failed to accomplish its goal. Ask yourself why you would trust an entity that is trillions in debt, with a failing currency system instead of yourself? I would rather be in control of my future instead of leaving it up to chance. Betting on the U.S. Government over yourself is the real gamble.

Prohibited Profits are everywhere and many of the world's newest billionaires are making their money in cryptocurrency and blockchain technology. My goal is that this book is an evergreen message about learning from historical patterns to predict future trends. However, I would be doing it an injustice not to discuss the current opportunity in crypto.

After reading this book, you have a few decisions to make. You can either return to business as usual, investing into the U.S. Casino. Or you can decide to invest into yourself and the future of technology.

There will always be naysayers that tell you Bitcoin and blockchain technology is a fad. They also said the internet was going away soon. If you think technology will send our society backwards, then you probably stopped reading a long time ago. If you believe that technology will only continue to advance, then start playing the game.

You don't have to quit your job tomorrow but commit to shifting your own identity. Once you finish this book, you are now an investor. Start to think like an investor and run your life like an investor would. Think about the you 5 years from now. Think about managing a multi-million-dollar portfolio because you decided to bet on yourself.

Start by reading books and finding a great mentor. If you can't afford to hire one, read all of your mentors' books and consume their content online. Start to get inside the mind of people you want to be like. You will become what you read, watch and talk about. If you let this consume you, you will learn, grow and gain confidence.

Next time you get a paycheck, decide that it's time to make a move. Don't invest your entire paycheck and put your family at risk. But invest what you can afford to lose. Remember, you don't need to invest a lot into the market to change your life.

If you start with $1000 and hit our 1000%+ 3 times, you will become a millionaire. Easier said than done, but I have watched it happen multiple times. As of writing this book, Crypto Wealth Coach has generated over 40+ millionaires from the crypto markets and counting.

3 years from now, it will be too late to take advantage of the limited window we are in now. Big banking money is flooding into the crypto markets. People are starting to understand inflation and the dangerous path our economy is heading down. The opportunity to claim your piece of the cryptocurrency fortune is now.

The beautiful thing about Prohibited Profits, is that there is always another opportunity in the future. But it's rare that an opportunity is available to the masses. For my entire life, Prohibited Profits opportunities were only available to some. Not the average guy like me. So I share this message urgently because I was in your position not long ago. I dreamed of better days and I dreamed of financial freedom.

One day I decided to do something about it, and I would encourage you to decide when that moment is. Eventually you will wake up to realize your adult life is passing you by and nothing has changed. The system is built to keep you on the hamster wheel forever, playing their game. It takes real courage, commitment and a bigger vision to bet on yourself.

I am honored that you would consider that mission for your life. If you need a guide along the way, you know where to find me.

Stay ahead of the masses,

Seth Maniscalco

Made in United States
North Haven, CT
19 May 2022

19329550R00093